The Passage of Time

Dalhousie Architectural Press
Faculty of Architecture and Planning
Dalhousie University
Halifax, Nova Scotia, Canada
dal.ca/archpress

Dalhousie Architectural Press Editorial Board
Christine Macy, Dean
Essy Baniassad
Sarah Bonnemaison
Brian Carter
Hans Ibelings
Frank Palermo
Michelangelo Sabatino
Susanne Marshall, Publications Manager

Shim·Sutcliffe — The Passage of Time
Editor: Annette W. LeCuyer
Designed by M1/DTW
Printed by Friesens

© 2014 Dalhousie Architectural Press
All Rights Reserved.
Printed in Canada
Reprinted June 2018

Library and Archives Canada Cataloguing in Publication

Shim-Sutcliffe — The Passage of Time
(Documents in Canadian Architecture)
ISBN 978-0-929112-63-3 (pbk.)

1. Architecture, Domestic–Ontario–Toronto–Designs and plans.
2. Architecture, Domestic–Ontario–Toronto–Pictorial works.
3. Architecture, Domestic–Ontario–Georgian Bay–Designs and plans.
4. Architecture, Domestic–Ontario–Georgian Bay–Pictorial works.
5. Shim-Sutcliffe Architects. 6. Shim, Brigitte, 1958–. 7. Sutcliffe, Howard.
I. Baniassad, Essy, writer of added commentary II. Title: Passage of Time.
III. Series: Documents in Canadian Architecture

NA7242.05S55 2014   728'.3709713   C2014-901792-8

Documents in Canadian Architecture

Shim·Sutcliffe — The Passage of Time

Contents

This publication presents two seminal projects by Shim·Sutcliffe in a detailed record of the process of their design and illustrated with drawings of exceptional quality. The two projects, images and narrative describe the culture and context that shape other projects that they have designed and are also presented along a time line. Together they form a record of some of the finest current architecture in Canada. As such, the publication makes an invaluable contribution to the documentation of Canadian architecture, broader architectural discourse and the study of architecture.

The buildings highlighted in this book are varied and unified. They exude a culture rather than a style that demands uniformity. It is a culture that affords freedom, suggests variety and brings vitality. The influence of this culture permeates the work at both physical and metaphysical levels. In each project, it unifies the material and the spiritual aspects — a defining quality of all notable works of architecture and art. Like a seasoned adult with a childlike directness of vision, the work combines the elemental simplicity of primal forms with the refinement of advanced designs.

To understand this work as a whole and appreciate the depth of its formative roots requires pause and silence. This is more difficult and perhaps delicate because, despite its evident consistency and continuity, this is a body of work that does not lend itself to any theoretical category or formal style. Here *DESIGN* is a unified and *CHOREOGRAPHED* assembly of materials within simple primal ideas. Each part is distinctly composed within that idea rather than being merely a part of a collection that is subject to a single overriding aim, function or formal construct. The entrance, handrail, stair, fountain and fireplace take on identity and become objects of attention that are rooted in their own making and function.

Beyond its formal attributes, I believe that the quality of this work flows from a broader design agenda than the singular conditions of each project. That agenda is one which it shares with other notable examples, such as the work of Alvar Aalto and Frank Lloyd Wright. It concerns the juxtaposition and resolution of long-standing dichotomies — regional/universal, part/whole, form/detail and issues that relate modernism and tradition. Each project rises above the factual and functional program of design and forms a step in an exploration of the architectonic potentialities of resolution and juxtaposition.

The interplay of a primal — 'significant'[1] — form and refined detail is evident in much of the work. This is a manifestation of the process of design as a patient search as expressed by Brigitte Shim and Howard Sutcliffe when they speak of the need "to posit a modernist tradition...to find balance not only between building and nature but also between lessons from the vernacular and ideas of modernism."[2] The result is the design and discovery of an architecture of 'ordinariness and light.'[3] Besides its evidently inherent delight, this body of work offers a rich gift for the study of longstanding questions about the nature of architecture and the process of design.

6   **Foreword** Essy Baniassad

1. *Shim·Sutcliffe*, The 2001 Charles & Ray Eames Lecture, MAP 9 (Ann Arbor: Taubman College of Architecture and Urban Planning), p. 50.
2. *Ibid.*, p 31.
3. Smithsons' development of the modernist discourse in *Ordinariness and Light* advances a splendid architectural counterpart that is detectable in the work of Shim·Sutcliffe. They highlight a way of working "without having to think in terms of larger systems" — a way of thinking that the Smithsons also referred to as "the Gothic mind." In addition, they outline their approach to materials — seeing materials for what they are: "the woodness of wood; the sandiness of sand" — and their view of the house as the primal architectural form in modern architectural discourse. Alison and Peter Smithson, *Ordinariness and Light*. (Cambridge: The MIT Press) 1970.

The foreword of the first edition of *Documents in Canadian Architecture* noted the objective of "producing documents that offer an insight into the process of design" and went on to confirm that the publications in that series would seek to record "the 'facts' and the products of the process: the sketches, drawings, and the end products." An initiative that also sought to raise international awareness of new architecture in Canada, the series focused on the need to make books which provided information for students and others with an interest in design. It was an approach that aimed to advance the study of architecture while avoiding the distractions of advertising and promotion that frequently haunt architectural publications.

The Passage of Time, reconfirms those objectives and uncovers ideas in significant contemporary Canadian architecture, which are the result of collaboration between Brigitte Shim and Howard Sutcliffe. This book is organized around two projects — a house in the city and a camp in the country. Each is modest in scale and both have been designed by the architects for their own use. In addition, they have been intimately involved with the construction of each building. Spanning over a period of nearly twenty years, the two houses support particular ways of living and present attitudes to life that have developed over time. They also reveal commitments both to urbanity and the wilderness — commitments that seem particularly Canadian.

The format of the book traces the evolution of the design of each house through drawings. Those drawings, ranging from early sketches to refined construction details, have been annotated with images of mock-ups and construction. Other photographs offer glimpses of the houses in use. The Laneway House in Toronto and Harrison Island Camp at Georgian Bay are part of a larger body of work by Shim·Sutcliffe. In an effort to track trains of thought, highlight processes of development and detect connections between projects, this book also seeks to locate the design of the two houses in that context.

8 **Introduction** Brian Carter

At a time when there is increasing encouragement to focus on the immediate present and an overwhelming emphasis on instant gratification, architecture can offer resistance. Not only do the design and construction of buildings take considerable time, but ideas develop and change through sustained sequences of projects. The context of a commission, the changing attitudes of a client, financial shifts, market influences, the availability of materials, advances in construction techniques, the seasons, land, weather and responses to buildings in use are just some of the forces that can shape architecture over time. And, as architects engage in many conversations, learn about materials, see other buildings, discover systems of assembly, review costs and oversee construction, they too refine their thinking.

This document reveals insights from close examination of the work of Shim·Sutcliffe and uncovers themes in the development of their work. This was a central interest when *Documents in Canadian Architecture* was initiated. It remains of prime importance in architecture today.

Conversations Brigitte Shim + Howard Sutcliffe

The essay on the following pages is compiled from a series
of conversations between Brigitte Shim, Howard Sutcliffe,
Brian Carter, Annette LeCuyer and Christian Unverzagt.

We live and work in the largest city in Canada. Toronto is situated on the Great Lakes, the largest group of fresh water lakes on earth. Ravines, which are part of the watershed feeding Lake Ontario, cut into the plateau where the city is located and are an important feature of its urban topography. The inhabitants of Toronto maintain an acute awareness of nature because of their proximity to these ravines, part of a remarkable ecosystem that clearly predates the city. Within two hours drive of Toronto, there is a range of other spectacular natural landscapes. In addition to the Great Lakes system, there are inland lakes in Muskoka and Haliburton, the Thousand Islands in the Saint Lawrence Seaway, and the prehistoric Canadian Shield. Our work seeks to highlight the distinctness of each of these terrains. The urban buildings and landscapes that we have designed reflect our belief in the need to increase the density of our cities. This is a reaction to the detrimental impact of suburban sprawl, which is consuming the best agricultural land in the country. Like the buildings we have designed in natural landscapes, our urban projects seek to intensify our relationship to nature.

Our house and studio are deliberately situated in the urban core of Toronto. Our house is on a former derelict site, and the studio was originally a garage and body shop. The regeneration of buildings and landscapes in the city should be an important dimension of all architectural practice. We always look beyond the current condition of a site to see its potential. The transformation of marginal urban sites is an important aspect of our practice. Such sites are often banal. The client for the synagogue that we designed in South Portland, Maine hired us because of our work at Ledbury Park in Toronto. We showed them photos of the park before our intervention. They wanted to create a sacred space on a dull piece of land surrounded by Dunkin' Donuts, the termination of a turnpike and a motel strip. When they saw how we had transformed Ledbury Park, they believed we could do the same with their rather unpromising site.

Formed by the retreat of glaciers 10,000 years ago and rivers running from the north to Lake Ontario, Toronto's ravines interrupt the city's grid. These deep, densely forested ravines support important ecosystems of water, wildlife and vegetation that act as "lungs" for the city.

Canada, a vast wilderness yet intensely urban, is one of the least populated countries in the world. An estimated 75 percent of Canadians live within 100 miles (160 kilometers) of the southern border, with most in cities. Toronto, located in this densely settled southern zone, has a population of 2.8 million and over 6 million in the greater metropolitan area, making it one of the largest and fastest growing cities in North America. Toronto is ranked by *The Economist* Intelligence Unit as one of the world's most liveable cities.

Our project for the Corkin Gallery is located in Toronto's Distillery District, one of the largest Victorian industrial complexes remaining in North America. Much of the 19th century structure of the building remained intact, including loadbearing brick walls at three foot centers, which originally supported enormous metal vats that were filled with pure spirits used to make hard liquor. The walls had vaulted openings to enable workers to move freely in the undercroft to drain lines and maintain pipework from the vats.

These found brick walls were retained and now make intimate gallery spaces for small works. Only in one area did we carefully remove selected brick walls to carve out the main gallery for large works of contemporary art. We designed a robust steel bridge that spans across the tops of the walls without touching them, so old and new are clearly articulated. The gallery library — housed on this floating bridge and enclosed with full height sliding panels of sandblasted glass — is like a lantern in the space. This wall of translucent glass can also be used for rear projection for video artists. Instead of whitewashing or homogenizing the existing building, the layers of old and new construction coexist and are legible.

The inaugural exhibition in the Corkin Gallery was the work of Thaddeus Howlonia, who had photographed the trees at Thoreau's Walden Pond. Each black and white photograph is ten feet high by three feet wide. Some of the trees are pure and untouched, while others show evidence of human interventions like graffiti and ladders embedded in the trunks. This work provides a parallel to our architecture's clear articulation of old and new. The relationship between human beings and nature that is important in Howlonia's art is also a critical engagement in our work.

The Corkin Gallery is in the former vat house of the Gooderham and Worts Distillery. Founded in 1832, Gooderham and Worts became the largest distillery in the world, but as industry declined after World War II, it was abandoned. The 13-acre Distillery District, which includes 40 buildings and 10 streets, was designated as a National Historic Site of Canada in 1988. It was purchased by Cityscape in 2001, who initiated its renovation and reuse as a new cultural precinct in the city.

Students see complex projects in architecture magazines and then are faced with a blank piece of paper or an empty computer screen. They often have little understanding of how to get from A to B. Consequently, for our own reference and for others, we document our design process and the evolution of ideas. We organize our drawings as a navigation tool that reflects how ideas develop — from site and landscape to elements like columns, fireplaces and handrails. We make 11x17 inch binders of drawings for each project that enable us to trace ideas from early sketches and design development through perspectives, permit sets, construction documents and shop drawings. Sometimes we have ideas that, for one reason or another, do not get built. However, we still record them because they were critical in getting to the final result. These documents enable us to see how ideas evolved for a particular project and to compare details from project to project.

Computer drawings do not speak about authorship as clearly as hand drawings. There is also an issue of scale. When you draw by hand, you draw the same thing over and over, at many different scales. Consequently, you know how big it really is. Because the drawing on the computer can be plotted at any scale, the real size of elements is not as well understood and scale becomes ambiguous. Of course, our office produces computer drawings, but the construction documents that we issue to contractors always include binders of freehand sketches produced during the design process. Sketches made during the contract are added to the documents as construction progresses.

We know from teaching architecture that students, when asked to build a model, will often take their CAD file to the laser cutter, which will cut out floor plates that they then stack like pancakes. If you believe that the section is important, you might ask, "Why would you make a model in that way?" We make many models throughout the development of each project, but they are not made by laser cutters or professional

13

"24 Tree Studies for Henry David Thoreau" Thaddeus Holownia, a British-born Canadian artist, received a Fulbright fellowship in 2001 to study Walden Pond. "Over the course of two years, he visited the area in all its seasons — a deliberate echo of the two years Henry David Thoreau spent at the site….His preoccupation with nature extends beyond its natural beauty, beyond the environmentalist's warning, to an understanding that the trees are a portrait of the human race."

Jane Corkin, *Walden Pond Revisited* (Toronto: Corkin Shopland Gallery) 2004, p. 8.

model makers. Because they are such a key part of our working process, we make them ourselves. Like our drawings, they reflect our thinking process, and they show the evolution of ideas.

Ironically, we have fewer models of the projects we have designed for ourselves than we do of our clients' projects. For our own houses, we are the shoemaker's children. We have worked through many projects together, so we are able to design in shorthand when we are experimenting on ourselves. We do this principally through drawings and full-scale mock-ups.

Many of our projects are houses. While they can be more complex than larger institutional buildings, houses are of a scale that enables us to take risks. We can test an idea and build it within a couple of years, and then we can inhabit the space. We spend time in all of our completed projects so that we can see how they work through the day and through the seasons. We also now have a number of clients who, several years after the completion of their initial commission, have come back to us for further projects. The Ravine Guest House was commissioned by the owner of the Garden Pavilion and Reflecting Pool, and studios were designed for both the Craven Road House and the Island House. These pairings, for the same client on the same property, but at different moments in time, create the opportunity for a conversation between buildings. These long-standing client relationships have been instrumental in the evolution of our work.

The nature of our practice is that, even as our commissions have grown in size and complexity, we continue to take on small, low budget projects because they allow us to experiment. Designing and building the Craven Road Studio, for example, enabled us to explore the quality of daylight from a narrow skylight. What we learned from that project

14

In the pastoral setting of the Thousand Islands in the Saint Lawrence Seaway, a large reflecting pool, together with a series of gardens and terraced green roofs, becomes the constructed landscape for a new pavilion — a tall, light room that forms the main living space of the Island House, completed in 2001. The client subsequently commissioned the design of a studio, which is a separate pavilion on the site that was completed in 2008.

was then elaborated and refined in subsequent projects. The reciprocities between one project and another are fundamental to our work. This ongoing series of experiments is more important than any single project, and it is central to our working method.

Everything we design is a prototype. We build mock-ups and then reflect on how they could be further developed at different scales and for different programs. While our small projects can be seen as built mock-ups, even the Integral House, although quite large, could be understood as a small scale experiment that subsequently led to a larger project for the Sisters of Saint Joseph of Toronto.

Architects typically do not experiment on themselves. They need to learn lessons from living in and experiencing the places that they design. However, they rarely do this because they are usually designing for someone else. We have always experimented on ourselves. Our own house in Toronto and the Harrison Island Camp at Georgian Bay are personal experiments. They have enabled us to explore and test a range of issues. The Laneway House, completed in 1993, is an urban manifesto. It was one of the earliest projects that we built, and it summarized how we wanted to live in the city. Harrison Island Camp, a project that we started in 2008, is a reflection and meditation on how we might live in nature.

We do not think about the Laneway House and Harrison Island Camp as isolated projects. It is more important to reflect on how they have evolved from and led to other projects, and how they fit into our body of work.

The Laneway House is a small dwelling that is a counterpoint to both the single family house and the high rise apartment tower — the dominant dwelling types in Toronto.

15

"The Garden Pavilion and Reflecting Pool — our first built commission — was completed in 1988. Over the years, we have designed and built a series of projects for that same client, including the Ravine Guest House and Reflecting Pool, completed in 2004. Each of these projects draws from earlier work and lays the groundwork for future schemes. Working with the same client over a long period of time has enabled us to develop a strong mutual understanding and refine ideas about the relationship of landscape, building, architecture and furniture."

It is a pavilion in a garden that seeks to intensify land use in order to support existing infrastructure. It builds upon the notion that everyone really wants to live in a village in the middle of the city. The existing neighbourhood infrastructure of schools, retail and transit would only improve if each neighbourhood were more dense. At the same time, we need to incorporate outdoor spaces — lush gardens, delightful courtyards, generous balconies and decks — that reconnect us to nature in the city.

We did not build our original scheme for the laneway site. It took several years to get permission to build, and by the time we received approval, our design thinking had evolved. The first version sought to capture as much space as possible. After the long municipal approval process, we had to go back to the City of Toronto to get approval for an adjustment to the original plan. The second version of the Laneway House looks similar to the original scheme, but it is fundamentally different. The section is more articulated. The connection to the garden is strengthened, and the relationship between inside and outside is more integrated. Through the evolution of the design, we refined our idea into a stronger and clearer concept, linking our thinking at the urban scale to the building and the detail.

Toronto's central neighbourhoods were mapped out in the 19th century, and our house is an infill project in a back alley that is embedded within the Victorian fabric of the city. In this dense urban context, a critical architectural consideration was how to bring light into the building interior. Our design strategy emerged from a knowledge of the typical Toronto house type. Toronto residential lots are narrow along the street frontage and deep, and the typical Toronto house has a side hall stair, which makes the narrow house even narrower. Our house has a center hall stair, so the living room enjoys the full width of the lot. Even though our lot is tucked into the laneway, its dimensions are nearly the same

16

"Ken Greenburg, who served as the director of Urban Design and Architecture for the City of Toronto, was an expert witness when the proposal for the Laneway House was reviewed by the Ontario Municipal Board. His testimony identified the development of housing on laneways as an untapped resource in the city."

as every property on the street — 17 feet wide and 45 feet long. The skylight and daylight above the stair make the interior space feel like an outdoor courtyard. This is in stark contrast to the typical Toronto house, which has light only at its narrow ends. We enjoy light at both ends and in the center of the house at the same time.

Because the Laneway House is small, our aim was to make one gracious room instead of many tiny spaces. We also wanted to have a direct relationship with nature — in this case a courtyard garden, which transforms our living room into an outdoor space surrounded by nature in the middle of the city. Our garden is very small, only 15 x 15 feet, but it is a lush and wonderful space that gives us pleasure every day.

Sections are very important in all of our projects. In the Laneway House, the section was developed to provide privacy. Seen from the outside, the solid wall at ground level is five feet high with a three foot translucent clerestory above. Inside, the floor of the main living space and garden is two feet below grade, creating a secluded oasis. The perimeter wall surrounding both house and garden is made of standard concrete block which, typically regarded as an exterior material, is pulled into the interior to unify this indoor-outdoor space. An unanticipated bonus of the clerestory is that, at night, the street light casts the shadow of the tree onto the translucent glass, so it brings to mind the abstractions of nature seen in Japanese prints.

The manipulation of light is a recurring preoccupation in our work — starting with clerestories and coffered wooden roofs and evolving into a series of explorations of thick walls. Craven Road Studio, the Synagogue for Congregation Bet Ha'am and the Integral House are all emphatically shaped by light. In each of these projects, substantial building elements are animated and also dematerialized by light.

17

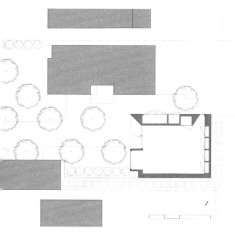

The walls of the Craven Road Studio, range from 8 to 36 inches in thickness. The linear skylight is a consistent width externally with uniform detailing around the entire perimeter. Internally, the junction of skylight to wall, which is furred out and clad with plywood, changes thickness to marry with each wall.

In Toronto, we are at 43.7°N latitude. Consequently, we are always seeking to amplify and expand winter light and deflect summer light. The Craven Road Studio was an important experiment in the use of daylight. Our client asked for a space with good natural light and no glare, as he wanted to house part of his working reference library and extensive collection of architectural photographs and posters. The studio is a single room with walls that modulate light. Each wall is a different thickness. The south wall, which sits on the property line, is the shallowest. The east wall includes book and file storage. The north wall incorporates outdoor storage for garden tools and equipment together with deep flat files for the studio. The west wall, which faces a small courtyard garden, is the deepest with a large bay window that can be occupied. The display walls are clad with painted gypsum board. Above, a one meter deep band of birch veneered plywood forms a slender linear skylight that washes each wall with light. The movement of the sun through the day, modulated by the thick walls, animates the space. Because of the skylight, it is rarely necessary to turn on the lights during the day, even during the long winter. At night, simple uplights illuminate the space. Throughout the year, and at all times of day and night, the studio has a luminous glow.

The Synagogue for Congregation Bet Ha'am in South Portland, which followed the Craven Road Studio, was conceived as walls of light. The congregation wanted a space that felt warm and inviting. In this project, light is captured and articulated to take on spiritual qualities. The sacred space is bounded by thick walls of light and shadow.

The first study model of the synagogue described the sculpting of light using a clerestory and skylight with a wooden baffle. Considering the site's latitude, we developed the section to amplify light, particularly during winter. The light conditions in the space are constantly changing. Depending on the time of day, light enters either in front of the wall

18

In the Synagogue for Congregation Bet Ha'am, the sacred space is animated by thick walls of light and shadow, together with the soft diffusion of light across the curved soffit of the roof.

or behind the baffle. The synagogue's side walls are canted, and the depth and angle of the east and west walls are different. The west wall is deeper, allowing it to capture the evening light, even in winter. In the Jewish tradition, the congregation turns to greet the sunrise and sunset and embraces them as part of their liturgy.

Our challenge was to design a sacred space on a modest budget. In Maine, there is still a strong boat building culture, so wood is an appropriate and economic material to use for cladding the building. The synagogue's exterior and interior are clad with cypress clapboard. Externally, the clapboard is lapped conventionally for weathering, and this produces typical shadow lines. Internally, the lapping is inverted so that the top edge of each board is exposed to receive the light. These fine lines of light are quite subtle and beautiful. It is a simple idea that works very well.

The first version of the building was more rational with vertical walls and a flat roof. As we developed the design, the walls splayed out to capture and emphasize the light. However, the roof remained flat. At a certain point, we began to use our study models to explore a curved soffit as a way of unifying the space. Instead of two walls with a void between, the space became a singular volume with the play of light on the curved soffit, as opposed to an even wash across a flat ceiling. This adjustment from a flat to curved ceiling was transformative.

A synagogue is an interesting building to design because there is no clear typology. The very first synagogue is thought to have been a tent in the desert. We imagined the Synagogue for Congregation Bet Ha'am as a tent between two strong walls. Ideally, the roof would have been a catenary structure, which would have been more tent-like, and we could have used the splayed walls to tie it back. We did explore that kind of structure,

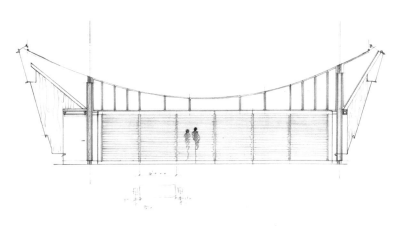

but for various reasons — including heavy snow loads and the budget — we ended up using inverted wooden bowstring trusses that are supported on longitudinal beams carried by columns concealed within the thick walls. The zone within the trusses houses both the mechanical plant and the ducts that service the space. The sanctuary and social hall are unified under this shaped roof.

In the Island Studio, experiments with light also incorporate colour. Every window in the studio has an adjacent plane of colour. For the high level windows to the main space — like two eyes looking out to the road — the canted ceiling is yellow. Other windows are complemented by a red wall and a blue clerestory. With the reflection from these primary colours, the quality of interior light in the space is unexpectedly intense.

Our client is not an artist, but is an avid art collector, so the studio is a place to hang art in a space that is separate from the house. When we designed the studio, we did not know which specific works of art the client wanted to display. The use of saturated colour in a studio is the opposite of the typical curatorial approach that advocates a neutral backdrop. The Island Studio brings out the intensity of colour in the art in a surprising and spectacular way.

The deep reveals of the openings in the Island Studio were further developed in the external wall of the Integral House. In that project, the relationship between inside and outside is modulated by a 24 inch thick wall comprised of sculptural wooden fins. The fins are fixed. However, because each fin is unique in shape and orientation, they interact with the sun to highlight awareness of changing light conditions. The movement of the occupant through the house, like the passage of the sun and the seasons, changes both

20

The south façade of the Island Studio is pulled out like the drawer of a chest, creating slot windows for views and a clerestory for daylight. In the depth of displacement between roof and wall, canted yellow painted panels diffuse the light, creating an intense warm glow on the exposed interior concrete.

"There are obvious references to Alvar Aalto in the Integral House, both in the relationship of orthogonal and organic formal languages and in the details. We did not think about it consciously when we were designing the project, but there are also many ways in which the scheme refers to the work of Le Corbusier. Like the Carpenter Center and the Millowners Association Building in Ahmedabad, the free plan is anchored by strong figural elements and enclosed by light modulating walls."

Integral House, Shim-Sutcliffe: The 2006 Martell Lecture (Buffalo: School of Architecture and Planning, University at Buffalo, SUNY) p. 39.

the quality and perception of space. Viewed from some angles, the perimeter fin wall appears to be solid, and from others it is totally transparent. The frames of the windows are concealed in the millwork so that, seen from the inside, the fin wall feels as if it is open to nature. The vertical fins, juxtaposed with the trees in the woods, can be read as representations of nature.

The Integral House informed the envelope of the building that we subsequently designed for the Sisters of Saint Joseph of Toronto. This scheme for a private hospital and assisted living facility is a long, curvilinear building that forms the backdrop for a chapel at the edge of a ravine in Toronto. The city's ravines tend to be private, so that when you drive along streets, it is impossible to know if there is a ravine at the rear of the houses. In the Integral House, we maintained clear views of the ravine from the street, so nature in the city remains part of the public experience.

This approach has been developed in a more emphatic manner in the project for the Sisters. The resident rooms face north and northeast, and the single loaded corridors are along the south and southwest façades, where vertical weathering steel fins provide sunshading and repetitive elements that support the rhythm of movement along the corridors. The fins are fixed, but as people inside and cars outside move along the building, the façade becomes interactive and its appearance changes. On the south elevation of the Sisters scheme, the windows between the fins are operable and, when used in tandem with the windows and doors of the residents' rooms, insure good cross ventilation in all interior spaces. The orientation of the building is an integral part of its sustainability agenda, which also includes geothermal wells, cisterns to collect rainwater, a green roof, solar hot water preheat and photovoltaic panels.

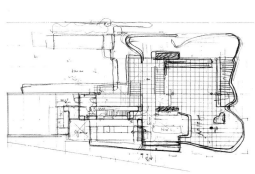

"...[It] is difficult to know how best to convey the essence of this house as a phenomenological matrix. Perhaps one may come closest by following the architect's own characterization of the work as an Aalto vase blown up to the size of a five storey building with more than ample ceiling heights.... [A]s the architects would be the first to admit, the spirit of Aalto rather than the letter is to be found everywhere in this work, newly inflected throughout but nonetheless there..... [The house] is above all else a *light modulator...*"

Kenneth Frampton

The Sisters saw the Integral House when it was under construction and appreciated the building's curvilinear form and its response to the ravine edge site. They did not want to live in a box, and the Integral House was an inspiration for them. The external wall of their building is another iteration of the idea of thick construction that manipulates light. However, the fins in the Sisters project are very different from those of the Integral House, both formally and materially. The Integral House fins are triangular volumes made of wood, while the fins of the Sisters building are thin folded planes that are weathering steel on one face and green polyester powder coated aluminum on the other. Although the fins are fixed in both projects, their position varies in response to the precise orientation of the façade.

Millworkers in Toronto fabricated the wooden fins of the Integral House, and we were able to work closely with them to develop and refine the details of the complex external envelope. For the Sisters project, we worked with the German fabricators Roschmann to develop the façade. A full-scale mock-up was built in Germany and was subjected to driving rain and wind at a testing center to evaluate its technical performance and to enable refinements before fabrication commenced.

While the new home for the Sisters of Saint Joseph of Toronto was being designed, a house for another client was being built in the eastern townships of Quebec. The House on Henry's Meadow is a further experiment in manipulating light. It combines a thick wall with a coffered skylight. The house is situated on the west side of Lake Memphremagog, a slender body of water that is 31 miles long and straddles the border between Quebec and Vermont. The design of the front facade is inspired by the stacks of firewood that are ubiquitous in this part of Canada. The log façade, framed by the clerestory of the lower floor and the skylight, appears to be detached from the ground and to float above

22

The siting and form of the Residence for the Sisters of Saint Joseph have much in common with Alvar Aalto's Baker House at MIT. In both, the serpentine plan, with the significant public space of the building held by the curve, mediates between the city and nature. The material vocabulary of the external envelopes — rough brick at Baker House and weathering steel for the Sisters' residence — is rugged. In the Toronto building, the vertical fins that shade the façade are a sandwich construction of weathering steel on one face and intense green polyester powder coated aluminum on the other. The fins of the Sisters of Saint Joseph — in contrast with the oak fins of the Integral House, each a unique triangular shape designed to appear monolithic — are a single repeated assembly of thin planes.

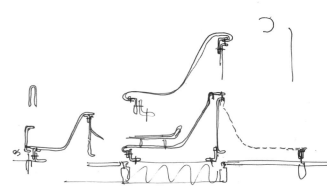

a reflecting pool. In contrast with the privacy provided by this front elevation, the rear of the house has panoramic views of the lake. The log wall, together with the coffered skylight and a weatherproof layer of translucent glass behind, faces west. In addition to letting light in, it acts as a screen to shade the house during hot summer afternoons. One of the clients for this house trained as an Islamic scholar, and the log wall — although inspired by stacks of local firewood — also brings to mind traditional wooden screens in Islamic cultures. From inside, the view of the logs is diffused by the glass. In winter, light is reflected from the snow, and the effect inside the house is striking. At night, the appearance reverses and the house glows like a lantern. The House on Henry's Meadow was also designed at the same time as the Harrison Island Camp.

We have built projects in many different places, but when we set out to select a site for our own cottage, it was very difficult. We had started looking for sites with a long list of requirements that included car access year round. We stayed in the House on Hurricane Lake and used it as a base to search for sites in the Haliburton area. In the end, we decided to locate on an island in Georgian Bay because the landscape there is so ancient, rugged and powerful. The geology of this unique landscape measures time over millions of years. It was an interesting journey for us to end up on the Canadian Shield. When you design something for yourself, you have to ask, "Where do we want to be? What landscape feeds the soul?"

In Canada, there are four distinct seasons. Consequently, the way our work frames and engages the landscape, both urban and natural, through the seasons and in all kinds of weather, is critical. Artists that include Tom Thomson and The Group of Seven's A.Y. Jackson are an important inspiration for us. They were the first landscape painters to actually go out and paint in the raw Canadian landscape. Their work portrayed its

The House on Henry's Meadow is a bar building flanked by two thick zones on the long facades. The public front of the house, which faces a shared meadow in the family compound, is closed and shielded by a log screen wall. Behind the logs, the thick zone incorporates vertical and horizontal circulation for the house. In contrast, the private rear façade facing the lake is fully glazed with sliding panels opening onto a continuous exterior deck.

ruggedness and exposure to the elements. These artists experienced the sublime qualities of that landscape and described it in a non-European way. Instead of painting pastoral images, they showed trees shaped by the west wind and evoked the unease of a blustery storm. Building on the work of the Group of Seven, Paterson Ewen is a contemporary Canadian artist whose work focuses on weather and atmosphere. His paintings represent cloud patterns or a rock rolling down a stream of water. In 1997, he asked us to design a new studio within his house in London, Ontario.

The Canadian Shield has been described as a stone necklace around Hudson's Bay. Its boreal forests, made up of native pines mixed with deciduous trees, are the lungs of North America. Much of the wildlife that we think of as Canadian lives in these forests. Harrison's Island, where our camp is located, is essentially ten acres of granite at the bottom tip of the Canadian Shield. The rock was gouged by retreating glaciers. Most trees are white pines and cedar, and there is a small grove of birches and a water meadow. All the trees are shaped by the prevailing west wind. We wanted to maximize awareness of the sculpting of the landscape by natural forces. The Harrison Island Camp, inspired by the work of the Group of Seven and Paterson Ewen, is centred around the creation of a delicate, articulated wooden tent on the Canadian Shield.

The idea of the tent is a statement about the relationship between human beings and nature, and it is expressed through the notion of lightness. We designed the camp just after the completion of the Integral House. After working for more than eight years on such a complex project, it was refreshing to design an elemental building in the landscape. There are parallel relationships between the Muskoka Boathouse, which was intense in its material palette and detail, and the Moorelands Camp Dining Hall, which had to be simple.

24

"Prior to [the formation of the Group of Seven], the art establishment's view of the northern Canadian landscape was that it was either unpaintable or too wild and uncouth to be worthy of being painted. ...[T]he Group came to be recognized as pioneers of a new, Canadian, school of art."

National Gallery of Canada, www.gallery.ca

ONMR, Ontario Centre for Remote Sensing E-1671-16352, centered at N51° 30', W93° 25.5', 25 May 1974. Bands 4, 5, 7. Coloured remote-sensing image 23 x 23 cm. Section of false-colour Landsat image, Red Lake area. Scale approximately 1:1,000,000.

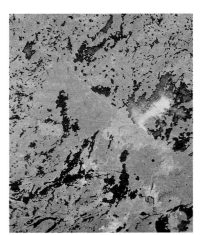

The Group of Seven, an informal association of painters, was formed in 1920 in Toronto by A.Y. Jackson, Lawren Harris, J.E.H. MacDonald, Arthur Lismer, F.H. Varley, Frank Carmichael and Frank Johnston. Tom Thomson, an advocate of painting the Canadian wilderness, was an inspiration for the movement.

"Two aspects of the Group contributed to their success then, and the same factors continue to keep their reputations alive now: their identification of 'The North' as a touchstone for Canadian sensibilities — 'the true north, strong and free'; and the conviction that their appeal to ordinary-thinking Canadians would be acceptable and accepted."

David P. Silcox, *The Group of Seven and Tom Thomson* (Toronto: Firefly Books Ltd) 2003, p 25.

The cabin feels like a big porch. When we are there, we live more outdoors than indoors. The idea of the porch is present in a number of our projects. It has developed through our rethinking of the vernacular and its adaptation for modern life. The design of the living room of the Island House — a cubic space with a clerestory that is surrounded by a reflecting pool — began by thinking about the qualities of a summer porch. The House on Hurricane Lake explores two interpretations of the porch — an elongated interior circulation space on the upper floor, where you can sit on a bench looking out over the lake, and a double height exterior area at ground level, which is the central space of the house. One porch extends horizontally and the other vertically.

The Harrison Island Camp is 1,100 square feet. The structure is comprised of a main central bay with cantilevers on each side, which form interior and exterior sitting areas. The elevation that looks out to the water is made predominantly of large sliding panels that open up to the landscape, while a long horizontal slot window frames views of the forest on the rear elevation. The windows, together with an operable linear skylight at the ridge of the roof, provide cross ventilation. They also blur the boundary between inside and out, making the entire cabin feel like a big porch. You can be under the roof, yet feel you are in the landscape experiencing the sun or wind or rain.

How to meet the ground is a critical consideration in the design of every building. On this site, it is particularly important. Ordinary construction in this region uses the Canadian Shield as a natural footing for concrete foundation walls. However, to us this seems disrespectful to the ancient Pre-Cambrian rock. We wanted to design in this place so that, over time, there would be no mark of human presence. The camp buildings have therefore been constructed as wooden tents. It is easy to imagine that they could be taken away and the site would return to its natural state. Our cabin touches the ground lightly,

The main living level of the House on Hurricane Lake hovers above the ground and is lifted into the tree canopy. Vertical and horizontal circulation, organized in a linear buffer zone on the landside of the house, links two volumes overlooking the lake — the living pavilion and the sleeping pavilion. These are separated by a vertical cut, which frames a terrace at ground level. While the rear of the house is clad with weathering steel, the glazed envelope on the south façade allows panoramic vistas of the landscape and interior vistas that pass through layers of interior and exterior space.

and it seeks to minimize possible long term damage to the rock. The foundations are connected to the bedrock using scaffolding screw jacks that are anchored into the Shield. The screw jacks can be adjusted to make a level base for the frame of the wooden tent. We have had opportunities to work in distinct Canadian landscapes, and this detail is particular to Georgian Bay. However, while Harrison Island Camp touches the ground lightly, other projects like the Garden Pavilion and the Laneway House are carved into the ground.

The Canadian Shield was formed by ice scraping and carving the ground as the last glaciers receded. The revealed landscape is raw and rugged, and it makes you think about time in a different way. For us, the landscape of Georgian Bay is a spiritual space. Erecting a wooden tent there is an acknowledgement that our time on this planet is fleeting. We are not building a monument. We are not defying nature. We are not being heroic. We are camping in an ancient landscape, which will be around for much longer than we will be.

Our house and cabin reflect quite different ideas about nature. Cottages symbolize the relationship of human beings to nature. This relationship has evolved over time. Our site in Georgian Bay is a unique piece of nature, and we bear the responsibility to be stewards of this pristine and remarkable environment. It is a privilege to own property on the Shield, and it becomes particularly important to look after it and ensure its ecology remains healthy. The site of the Laneway House embodies a different kind of environmental stewardship. It was a empty lot with abandoned cars, a piece of waste ground that nobody wanted. Our house remediates the site to create a place in the city. Nature is incredibly aggressive, both in Georgian Bay and in the city. If buildings are not looked after, nature will quickly take over — from mould and ants to material decomposition.

The lower level of the House on Hurricane Lake, where guest quarters are located, sits firmly on the ground on a plateau that is cut into the sloping site, and the main living quarters are above. The double height exterior void, which marks the entrance, is anchored by a chimney that serves both the interior fireplace of the living room above and an open air hearth for the terrace below.

These two projects explore our dynamic relationship to nature. The Laneway House has a tiny courtyard garden, which offers a fabricated vision of nature in the city. In the Harrison Island Camp, we are surrounded by nature. Modern architecture promoted the myth of man versus nature. It envisaged an architecture that controlled nature by framing it through the big window. This polarized relationship is changing.

At the Harrison Island Camp, we are within nature, which is a more subtle relationship. When we are there, we are outside most of the time, so our awareness of nature is more profound. We are much more sensitive to day and night, wind and rain and nature's smells. Because it is a camp, the structures are ephemeral and the space between rooms is actually outside. We are sensitized to being in nature, instead of being in a house just looking out at it.

In contrast, the House on Hurricane Lake was explicitly designed for a city dweller who does not want to go out into nature. As a result, the main living floor is lifted up off the ground, and the house is designed to feel like a treehouse. When it came to designing our own cottage, we are much closer to the ground, both literally and figuratively.

In the House on Hurricane Lake, as with the Weathering Steel House, sightlines and movement through a sequence of spaces are fundamental to the experience of the place. As you move along the length of these houses, you see inside, outside, inside, outside. This layered condition is also present in the cantilevered outer bays of Harrison Island Camp. However, because our cabin is more camp-like, all circulation is outside. In the long term, the current bedroom will become the dining room to make the main cottage totally public. Eventually, all sleeping accommodation will be in separate little buildings. The Ravine Guest House, Craven Road Studio and the Island Studio are all essentially one room buildings.

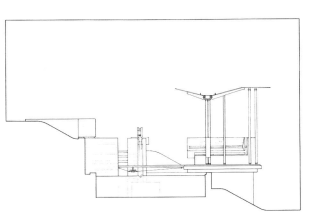

"[The Garden Pavilion is]…a finely articulated and exquisitely wrought miniature landscape of granite gravel terraces, concrete retaining walls and pools. Set within this highly articulated composition is the sandblasted roofed pavilion of weathering steel, under the overarching branches of the mature wood lot…..[T]his pavilion, a primitive hut, is variously and ambiguously supported by a grove of ten slender colonnettes which both screen and contribute to the ornamental and rhetorical character of the roof."

Michael Milojevic, "Time Constructions – An Architectural Lineage of Weathering Steel," *Praxis* (Volume 1, Issue 1) 2000, p.4.

The promenade is always important, even in a small project like the camp. Moving from water to land is a key part of the experience of the place. The sequence from dock to rock and then along a 300 foot long boardwalk is an elongated and extended promenade that is entirely outdoors. In contrast, the Laneway House is in the middle of a city block, and the path to the front door is direct. Because the house fills the entire site, circulation is internalized, compressed in plan and developed in section. You move down to the garden and up to the light.

The Laneway House is part of an urban ensemble. It is not an object in itself, but is embedded in the fabric of the city. In the Harrison Island Camp, the buildings read both as distinct objects and as an ensemble. At present, the main cabin and the wash house are built, together with a 200 square foot guest cabin, which is a variation on the cottage. The sleeping cabins will all be different. There is so much rock on the island that we are also planning to make a stone building, which will be a studio. We have collected an enormous pile of stones that we will use to build a granite cube.

Making small buildings is a traditional pattern of settlement in the landscape of the Canadian Shield. In this context, the spaces between buildings are as important as the buildings themselves. No matter how big the building, it is always tiny compared to the vast scale of the landscape. This differs from other places, where the scale of the landscape is more modest.

Like many of the traditional camps in the region, the Harrison Island Camp is largely self-sufficient. The wash house is behind the cabin and faces north. It cantilevers out from a little cliff above swampy ground, and it is pinned back to the rock. It includes a bath, shower, composting toilet and small utility room. While the south elevation is clad

The exterior colonnade of the Weathering Steel House is part of a series of transitional elements — low walls, decks and steps — that connect building and landscape. Large steps that run parallel to the reflecting pool and swimming pool lead to the outdoor deck and to the untouched natural landscape of the ravine beyond.

The Ravine Guest House — like the Laneway House — is anchored internally by the hearth and externally by a pool of water. Large glazed doors open generously, blurring the boundary between the interior and nature.

with wood to provide privacy from the house, the entire north elevation is glazed and opens up to the forest. The shower is essentially an outside shower, although there is an insect screen. Half the roof area of the wash house will be covered with solar panels, and there is an area of louvers in the middle with solar collectors for the hot water tank. Water is pumped from the lake, and we have grey water pits for the shower and sink, which will filter the water we use, enabling it to eventually percolate back into the lake. It is a utility building in more than one way. You can go there to shower or bathe, and at the same time, the building will provide energy for the whole site. The cottage is only used during the summer. Over the whole year, we can be net positive in terms of energy consumption. We pay for the initial investment and the Ontario power provider will pay over a period of 20 years for power returned to the grid. The cabin uses minimal resources and, even when we are not there, the site will be working as an energy generator. Consequently, we will give back more than we take.

All building materials had to be transported to the dock at the edge of Georgian Bay by truck and then loaded onto a barge to be taken to the island. Then everything had to be unloaded onto the island and carried by two people to the site. Consequently, the weight of building materials was a concern, and lightness relative to handling and manoeuvrability was critical. During the design process, every component was scrutinized and reviewed. The cabin is thin. To reinforce its tent-like quality, the cabin is elemental.

The design of the cabin is an experiment about prefabrication. It would not have been possible for us to design it without having previously designed the Dining Hall at Moorelands Camp in Haliburton. That project made us think about how to build economically on remote sites.

The Craven Road Studio was completed ten years after the house for the same client. In order to comply with planning regulations for secondary structures on residential lots, the size and placement of the studio on the urban site are the same as a two-car garage. The 'garage door' — a large glazed opening with external shutters that is set in the deep reveal of the thick wall — opens to a compact courtyard garden that unites house and studio.

All the components for the cabin were fabricated in a shop in Toronto in a controlled environment. We wanted the assembly to be very thin, so the structure is minimal. The columns are brake-formed steel plates. They are exposed externally but are not evident within. They carry a long box beam made of 2 x 4s, which in turn picks up the steel primary structure of 2 x 2 inch rectangular hollow sections with straps that span the central bay. It is an amazingly light structure. The steel straps were predrilled for site-bolted connections. Structural insulated panels are used for the floors, walls and roof. Floor and wall panels are flat, while the roof panels are curved. To minimize wastage, this panel system was designed on a 4 x 8 foot module — the basis of construction in North America. Windows are fiberglass, which is much lighter than glass. Here it was feasible because this is a seasonal camp building that is not winterized. The walls and roof are clad with sheets of weathering steel. In this context, our use of weathering steel is perhaps counterintuitive to the idea of lightness. However, although it is heavy, it appears to be light because it is thin. We have used weathering steel in many projects because, as a material that reacts to the atmosphere and changes in appearance over time, it has a close relationship to nature.

In the fabricator's workshop, we built a full-size mock-up of one bay of the cabin's structure and envelope to test all of the details. We worked closely with our structural engineer to make the cabin as light as possible, both in appearance and in actual weight. Because we were building for ourselves, we could take risks. We could try things because we were prepared to make adjustments if necessary. Building for yourself is a good way of testing the limits of what is possible.

We decided to use prefabricators from Toronto for the cabin because timing was a factor, as well as affordability, quality and control. The skylight, which is standard off-the-shelf

30

"During the summer of 2011, we installed solar collector panels on the roof of our office in Toronto. To date, the installation is operating at 120% percent of the predicted capacity. All power produced goes to the grid, and Shim·Sutcliffe receives a credit of $500 per month from Ontario Hydro — equivalent to nine trees saved — which covers approximately 25% of the electricity consumed by the building and office computers and equipment. The estimated payback period is eight years. The installation provides a full-scale working mock-up that the office can monitor and evaluate year round in preparation for the solar collectors that are planned for the roof of the wash house at the Harrison Island Camp."

Located on a peninsula in the Haliburton Highlands, Moorelands Camp provides a summer wilderness retreat for economically disadvantaged urban children. Three hours north of Toronto, the remote site is accessible only by boat. To capture the spirit of the camp, the building is conceived as a simple wooden tent. To make the largest span with the smallest components, the primary structure of glulam columns and trusses with steel tension cables is enclosed with 2x4 light wood framing. Construction commenced at the end of August and was completed in time for the next summer camp season. The carpenters lived on the site through the winter.

greenhouse glazing, runs the entire length of the cabin. It cost only $1,000, including all operating hardware. We had access to metal and wood fabrication shops in Toronto, and we built all the components during the winter months, when things are quiet on building sites. In the spring, everything was moved up to Georgian Bay.

There no longer seems to be any kind of intrinsic vernacular craft tradition in the vicinity of Georgian Bay. The building industry is clearly stratified, and by the time you drive an hour and a half north of Toronto, the construction culture is pragmatic and buildings are invariably banal. In that context, prefabrication was an alternative strategy for achieving a more refined building that was also affordable. It provided discipline to the design process and enabled us to take advantage of the high levels of craftsmanship available in a large metropolis. We had long term collaborative relationships with all the key fabricators, and these had developed and evolved through working together on multiple projects. We coordinated the fabrication of components in Toronto. A builder from Toronto did most of the site assembly, and we finished it off.

The construction timetable was affected by the climate and the fact that the site is inaccessible in winter. The people who did the work on site lived in tents on the island during construction, which took place over several summer seasons. It takes three hours to drive from Toronto to Georgian Bay, and then it is another fifteen minute boat ride to the island. A van filled with construction material equals four boat trips, so it can take a whole day to get materials onto the island.

Prefabrication is a popular topic in contemporary architecture, yet in some ways it seems at odds with the density of detail and refinement in our work. However, in contrast to standard prefabricated houses, which tend to be generic boxes, we chose to expand the

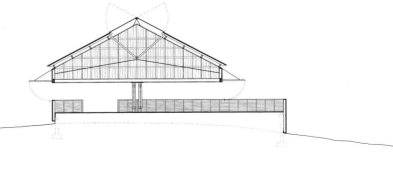

potential of prefabrication as an alternative construction strategy for remote sites. The Harrison Island Camp did not come fully assembled on a truck and get dropped on the site. Instead, the scale of elements is small so that each piece can be guided to its final place on the site by hand. While most prefabricated dwellings conform to a predictable checklist of modernist criteria, this cabin at Georgian Bay seeks to be more particular. Its components are not generic. They are more articulated than a standard prefabricated product.

We have designed furniture, fittings and light fixtures for many of our projects. They are as important as the architecture because each one is a small experiment exploring materials and their assembly, albeit at another scale. Our first project, the Garden Pavilion and Reflecting Pool, explored the integration of architecture, landscape, furniture and lighting. We have continued to address these issues in all of our projects in different ways.

For example, the roof of the Harrison Island Camp is similar in design concept to our HAB Chair, which is a wooden shell with steel straps. Both use steel plate that is flat instead of on edge, which is an atypical structural solution. The chair and the cabin also share the idea of folding and bending, and the parts that people touch are made of wood, which is warm and inviting.

For us, combining architecture, landscape design and industrial design is fundamental to the way we think about shaping space. In the Laneway House, we designed the garden and fountain, the fireplace and fire grate, the dining table and an articulated column. The light fittings and the HAB Chair that we designed for the Muskoka Boathouse are now products that are manufactured and distributed internationally by Nienkämper. They have been followed by numerous light fixtures and pieces of furniture designed for subsequent projects. For the synagogue, in addition to the light fittings in the sanctuary and social

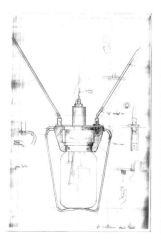

"In order to gain the requisite detailing experience to meet their own expectations, Shim·Sutcliffe uses small-scale test pieces, fine tuning their material choices and fabrication ideas. These are subsequently integrated into their architectural/ landscape projects....Like Lewerentz or Scarpa they insist on an intuitive and hands-on working method in which the design is the product of exhaustive discussions and a continual exchange of knowledge with trades- and craftsmen."

Michael Milojevic, "Time Constructions – An Architectural Lineage of Weathering Steel," *Praxis* (Volume 1, Issue 1) 2000, p.46.

hall, we designed all the liturgical elements — reading table, ark and ner tamid. We are now working on the design of a stackable chair for the synagogue and several pieces of furniture for the Integral House.

Industrial design has enabled us to experiment with innovative ways of using and assembling materials and to work at a human scale that is immediate and direct. It is the same kind of thinking that goes into realizing architecture. Our cabin might be thought of as a large piece of industrial design or a small piece of architecture. While we do not think of the cabin as a product like a light fixture or chair, we have already used similar construction components and systems in the design of the House on Kawagama Lake in Haliburton. The steel strap structure and external envelope in that project are essentially the same system used in our cabin, but the Kawagama Lake house is insulated for year round use, with a much thicker roof assembly.

Because it is designed to be occupied in all seasons, it was not appropriate to think of the House on Kawagama Lake as a tent in the woods. In this part of Ontario, there is also no strong vernacular tradition. However, there is a desire for a rustic cottage retreat, something that is distinctly different from urban life. In this case, the clients live in England and, for them, this retreat defines what it means to be Canadian.

Material choices are critical in all of our projects. On the Laneway House, we worked with the artist Margaret Priest to develop the material and colour palette for the project. We used concrete block and wood for their intrinsic texture and colour. The applied colours are red, white and black, which is an almost universal primitive palette signifying blood, life and death. The deep red Jatoba wood floor of the sunken living room has an earthy quality. Warm ochre Marmorino Veneziano plaster is applied on the fireplace chimney,

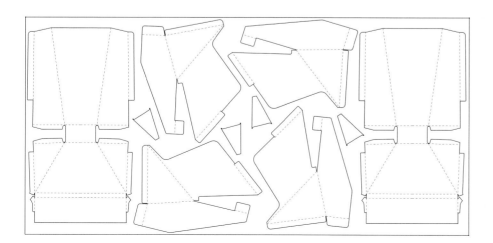

a luminous volume in the center of the house which is complemented by the blackened steel of the fire grate.

In contrast, Harrison Island Camp is made of wood, steel and weathering steel – materials that we have used on many projects, working repeatedly through drawings, models and mock-ups to refine construction details. Internally, the palette of applied colour in the cabin is shades of green, gray and black that are drawn from the Georgian Bay landscape. Flashes of bright green in the house are seen relative to, and in contrast with, nature. Inside, everything in the zone of the human body — from the floor up to a height of seven feet — is all natural material and colour, while the floor plane and roof volume are stained black. The body occupies the space between the black surfaces, which is also the zone of light and view.

The interior materials of the cabin highlight the contrast between darkness and light, and they oscillate between the primitive and the modern. In the House on Hurricane Lake, darkness and light played out differently than we had imagined. In the original scheme, the roof volume was to be stained black on the interior, and there was a slot to bring in daylight. During construction, there was a long discussion about whether the wood should be stained or not. In the end, we decided to keep the natural colour of the wood. As a consequence, when we designed our cabin, we decided deliberately to make the roof volume dark with a slot of light at the ridge. This play between dark and light, ancient and modern, primitive and refined is critical on the rugged site at Georgian Bay.

The Harrison Island Camp is inspired by the long-standing tradition of the vernacular shed. The old camps in the Georgian Bay region were wooden sheds stained with pine

34

The House on Kawagama Lake is sited in a mature forest on a sloped site looking north to the lake. The continuous skylight along the ridge of the weathering steel roof brings light into all rooms and emphasizes the space within the cottage as a light filled "clearing" in the forest. This is in direct contrast to the shaded nature of the dense forest surrounding the building. From within, views up the hill focus on the forest floor, while those down the hill are directed to the shoreline of the lake.

tar inside and out. They were dark and brooding dwellings. We wanted that darkness, and we wanted our cabin to be permeated by the smell of pine tar — a powerful scent that reminds us of those old cabins. We spent a lot of time and energy finding pine tar, which we eventually got from Sweden. The interior of the cottage was like the vernacular sheds for about two weeks, but we were disappointed when the smell then evaporated. No doubt this was a consequence of technical advances in the chemistry of paints and stains, but it was maddening! We have visited ancient Norwegian stave churches, which also have that distinctive scent, though perhaps that is the result of many coats of pine tar applied over the centuries. For us, the sense of smell is tied to the archaic.

The Laneway House is inward looking and contained, while the cabin emphasizes the absence of containment. Both the house and the cabin are long, thin buildings. However, the house opens on the short ends, while the cabin opens on the long sides. The conditions of dwelling in the two projects and how we occupy the space are totally different. In the urban Laneway House, the clerestory admits light but does not allow view. The interior of the house is luminous. Views outside are contained by the perimeter wall and focus close in on the dense verdant garden. The cabin, in contrast, is dark inside in order to focus on powerful distant panoramic views of nature.

The horizon line is important in both houses, but our relationship to it is fundamentally different. In the Laneway House, the horizon line is the boundary between wall and clerestory. The view is focused down into the garden instead of up into the messy urban laneway. At one point, a piece of glass in the clerestory had to be replaced, and when it was removed, the whole house was transformed. We could see down the laneway and suddenly felt totally exposed.

"…[W]eathering steel (also known as Cor-Ten or Weatherloy) is designed to rust to an unstable and uneven colour that ranges from orange-red to a black-aubergine. This colouration develops when soluble and gelatinous salts and sulphates leech out of the rust film, generating white or yellow lines that move with successive showers and according to the seasons….

…Surface weathering, oxidation, and the accumulation of marks of use (and misuse) refer to the fourth dimension, the object's existence, time, and, like the facial/body scar, convey historical detail. Weathering steel, of all contemporary building materials, most poignantly expresses the constructive passage of time."

Michael Milojevic, "Time Constructions — An architectural Language of Weathering Steel," *Praxis* (Volume 1, Issue 1) 2000, p.44.

"Working with the same material in different ways over an extended period of time is important in order to gain a deep understanding of its properties and potential."

Shim·Sutcliffe, The 2001 Charles & Ray Eames Lecture, MAP 9 (Ann Arbor: Taubman College of Architecture and Urban Planning) p. 77.

The site section of the Laneway House highlights the horizon — what you see and what you do not see. This perception was critical to the way we conceptualized the design of the house. When you enter, your eye is at the level of the clerestory band of sandblasted glass. It is not until you descend into the living room that you are in the world of the garden, which is disconnected from the city, creating a physical and psychological oasis.

At the camp, the horizon line is just above floor level, where the house opens out to light and view. There is a datum at table height that runs through the entire building, which echoes nature — the sky above, earth and water below. We had a large piece of Connemara marble, which we have used to make a dining table. This moss green, lichen-coloured plane of polished marble represents nature and marks the horizon line. It is a striking contrast to the raw and rugged landscape outside.

We have also incorporated other representations of nature in the cabin, which are experiments to see if we could contribute to an architectural tradition and heighten awareness of the place. Country houses in Japan or villas in Italy historically included representations of nature inside the dwellings. They are in nature, and views framed by windows are juxtaposed with framed paintings and frescoes of nature. Likewise, in Philip Johnson's Glass House, there is an easel that holds a 17th century landscape painting, which is positioned so that you can view it while simultaneously looking out to the woods. It is perverse, but interesting.

In the National Gallery of Canada in Ottawa, there is a fragment of a Georgian Bay cottage that has been pulled apart and reinstalled on the gallery walls. It was made by several of the artists in the Group of Seven, and it is the interior of a cottage painted. The cottage was in nature, and then it became a canvas for the artists' representation of nature.

36

"But for all that Johnson did it is inevitably to the Glass House that one returns. His identity is so tied into this place that the structure feels less like a work of architecture than an autobiography written in the form of a house, much like Jefferson's Monticello or Sir John Soane's Museum in London — amazing buildings in which the architect was the client and the client was the architect, and the goal was to express in built form the preoccupations of a life....

The Glass House itself, built in 1949, is essentially one room.... From inside, the carefully manicured landscape visible through the glass functions as an enclosure, and the ironic illusion is superb: The vistas tell the occupant that he is open to the whole world, while in truth there is no world outside at all, just the elegantly arranged landscape that is as much a part of the house as the furniture. The line between inside and outside becomes both visually and conceptually ambiguous...."

Paul Goldberger, "Introduction," *The Glass House* (New York: Skira Rizzoli Publications, Inc.), 2011, p.2-3.

We have made two panels, which are at opposite ends of the living space in the Harrison Island Camp. These pieces transform leftover materials from the construction site into representations of nature. Like a Japanese woodblock print, one panel represents falling rain. Japanese prints often depict rain, snow and wind. Our panel, "Navigational Channels," which shows rain falling over islands in Georgian Bay, describes the elusive atmospheric conditions and the horizon line.

The other panel, "Night Sky," is made of construction plywood that had been lying around outside, so it is gray and weathered. It was originally the platform of the tent where the builders lived during construction. It is full of knots, which reminded us of the stars in the night sky. Tiny mixing bowls, painted on the inside and nailed to the plywood, become the constellations.

In the Laneway House, the fireplace inside and the fountain in the garden are the anchors of the main living space. The fire signifies inhabitation, and the water and garden are representations of nature. In the same way, the cabin is anchored by the fireplace inside and water outside, while the two paintings in the cabin take on the task of representing nature abstracted and intensified.

The house and cabin view nature in different ways and, in both, the detailing of the windows is critical. When we built the Laneway House, we specified custom designed mahogany windows, with a large full-height pivoting window that could open to connect the living room to the garden. The fabricators told us that it would not work. However, because the house was to be our home, we assured them that we would not sue and suggested, "Let's build it so we can see how it works." It has worked well for two decades. We have refined this window prototype, and it has become an integral part of many subsequent projects.

37

Philip Johnson purchased *Burial of Phocion,* painted in 1648 by Nicolas Poussin, and placed the painting in the Glass House in 1949, shortly after construction was complete. "The significance of *Burial of Phocion* lies… in the painting's composition. The classical landscape depicted mirrors Philip Johnson's approach to the Glass House landscape — an environment that appears natural yet is cultivated. Johnson spent his entire life editing and cultivating what became over 47 acres of the Glass House site that includes fourteen structures, mature trees and plantings, as well as the stonewalls scattered throughout the property from its previous farm use."

Press release from the National Trust for Historic Preservation, 15 January 2008

Insect screens on windows are essential in the places where we work, but they are typically visually obtrusive. While designing the Laneway House, we developed a detail where the frame of the insect screen is recessed, so it is not seen. In order to realize that detail, we collaborated with the millworker who built all the windows.

The recessed frame makes an amazing difference, and this detail has subsequently been refined through a number of projects. For the Island House, the client wanted a screened porch. Using this same detail, we turned the entire living room into the porch. It was designed with full-height sliding glass doors at the corners and insect screens with recessed perimeter frames and no corner frame. The entire space can be opened up to capture breezes from the Saint Lawrence River. However, you are still aware of the insect screens, because they are close to the plane of the windows.

In the Harrison Island Camp, there is now a deep space between window and insect screen. This depth minimizes the visual presence of the screens. The corners, where the cantilevered bays jog in and out, are made by two wood framed sliding windows, one on each face of the corner. The insect screens are set three inches out from the face of the external wall, while their perimeter frames are recessed and there is no frame at the corner. When the sliding windows are open, one enjoys an uninterrupted landscape view while still being protected from insects, which is critical. From the exterior, the insect screens read as a volume. Inside they seem to disappear. We can open either one or both sliding windows, or close the whole assembly. We have used our own projects to continually experiment and refine elements. We can test the visual impact and performance of details. We live with them so that, on the next project for a client, we can continue the process.

The living room of the Island House is intimately connected with nature. It is designed as a porch with sliding glass panels that allow for generous light, views and cooling breezes. The primary structure is pulled away from the pavilion's corners and windows are detailed so that, when open, the clerestory and roof seem to float. Amplified by the reflection of light off the water, this pavilion absorbs light during the day and glows at night.

The passage of time enables us to develop and refine schemes and their details, influencing our choice of materials and shaping our attitude to environmental stewardship. The passage of time is an important aspect of architecture. In all of our work, we grapple with the issues of time, use and inhabitation — opening and closing, responding to the seasons, day and night. Both houses change quite dramatically from day to night. The garden of the house is beautiful in very different ways in summer and winter. The camp is open and in use in summer, closed and dormant in winter.

Both house and cabin were experiments in design and construction. They continue to be laboratories about life, specifically about our life and about how we think about the world. And as we live in them, they in turn take on their own life.

"The idea I have of a house is the idea of a complicated machine, in which every day something breaks down: a lamp, a tap, a drain, a lock, a hinge, a socket, and then a cylinder, a stove, a fridge, a television or video; and the washing machine, or the fuses, the curtain springs, the security bolt....

When there is a garden, the grass is growing menacingly, whatever free time you may have is not enough to deal with the madness of nature: fallen petals and legions of ants invade thresholds of doors....

Living in a house, in a real house, is a full-time job. The house owner...commands all the arts and professions, he is a specialist in physics, in chemistry, he is a lawyer — or he does not survive. He is a telephonist and receptionist, he calls at all hours, getting hold of plumbers, carpenters, bricklayers, electricians, and then he opens the front door to them...goes along with them submissively; because he depends on them....

This is why I consider owning, maintaining and renovating a house to be a matter of heroism. In my opinion there should be an order of the Guardians of Houses and every year the appropriate honour and a high financial award conferred.

But when all this effort of maintenance is not apparent, when the wholesome aroma of wax in a house, which is otherwise well-ventilated, is mingled with the perfume of flowers from the garden, and when in it we, irresponsible visitors...feel happy and forget our worries as barbarian nomads, then the only possible prize is one of gratitude, of silent applause: a moment of pause, looking around, losing ourselves in the golden atmosphere of an Autumn interior at the end of the day."

Alvaro Siza – Writings on Architecture (Milan: Skira editore) 1997, pp. 47–51.

Laneway House

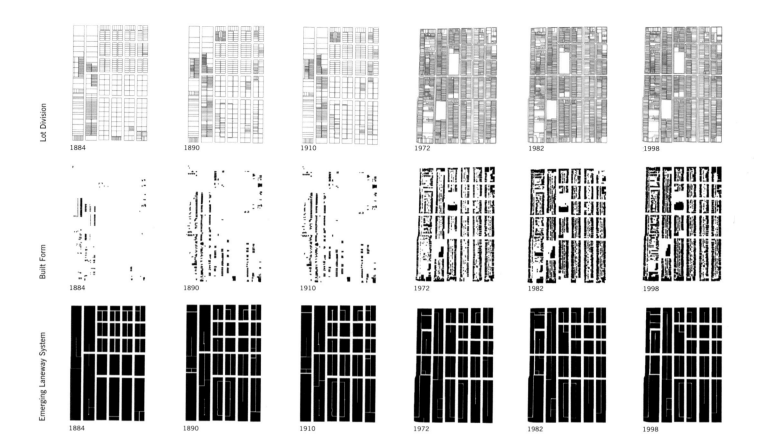

Lot Division
1884 1890 1910 1972 1982 1998

Built Form
1884 1890 1910 1972 1982 1998

Emerging Laneway System
1884 1890 1910 1972 1982 1998

"Since the....ascendancy of Koolhaas and his fellow avant-gardists in academic urban design circles, we have seen a different theoretical discourse rise to prominence, one that focuses on large as opposed to small-scale projects, that privileges urban infrastructure instead of urban fabric, and which impatiently prefers dramatic, and precipitous urban change, to incremental urban transformation."

Foreword by George Baird, *Site Unseen* (Toronto: University of Toronto Faculty of Architecture, Landscape and Design) 2004, p. 8.

"Developers keen on maximizing street frontage viewed the laneway as a device for organizing commercial and residential types along the perimeter of the block. In the inner-block, it provided a physical break for an otherwise congested arrangement. The laneway emerged with the simultaneous formation of the block, the urban lot and its associated housing. Together, they were an intrinsically related and highly effective set of components for maximizing block density."

"Insuring ideal street frontage meant that the daily realities of servicing were pushed behind the house to the laneway. Typically found in working neighbourhoods, the laneway was an indispensable component, providing the opportunity for kitchen garbage and outhouse waste removal. In wealthier homes and small businesses, its function expanded to accommodate live-in staff in coach houses, and the horse and carriage."

Brigitte Shim and Donald Chong (editors), *Site Unseen* (Toronto: University of Toronto Faculty of Architecture, Landscape and Design) 2004, p. 15.

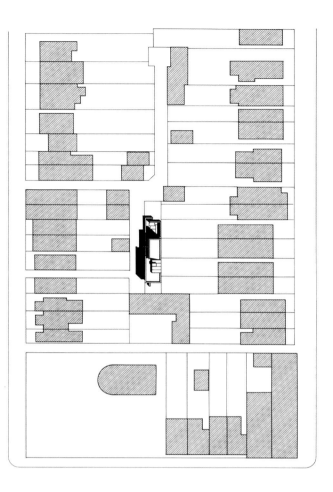

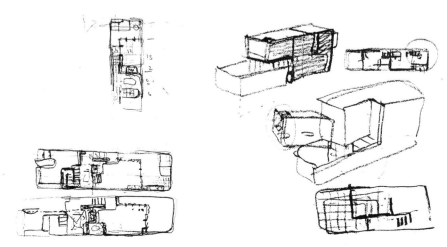

"In the last decade, the laneway —
or alley — has demonstrated…the
opportunity to generate thoughtful and
regenerative architectural insertions in
Toronto….[T]he city's laneway systems
are recognized as a legitimate and
potentially vast urban 'resource' offering
a new, incremental urbanism."

Brigitte Shim and Donald Chong (editors), *Site Unseen*
(Toronto: University of Toronto Faculty of Architecture,
Landscape and Design) 2004, p. 2.

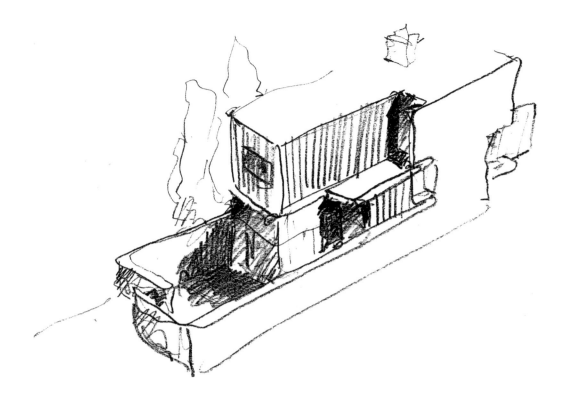

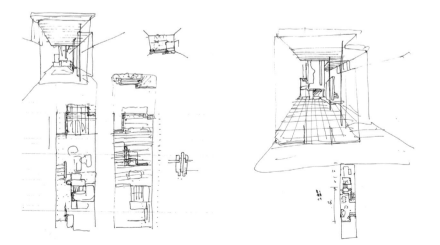

"The external wall of the Laneway House was originally detailed to be a 16-inch thick cavity wall, with two wythes of CMU and insulation in the cavity. However, this resulted in walls that were too thick for a house that, built to the maximum footprint allowed, was just 17 feet in overall external width. Therefore, we changed the wall construction to a single 8-inch thick wythe of reinforced CMU with 4 inches of external insulation and finish (EIFS)."

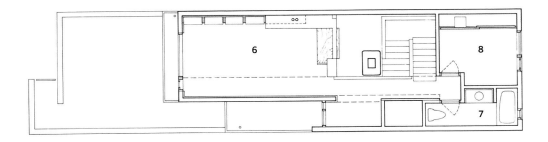

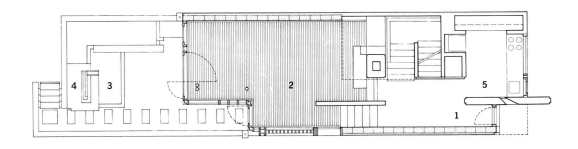

0 1　　　5　　　10'

1 Entry
2 Living / Dining
3 Pool
4 Fountain
5 Kitchen
6 Library
7 Bathroom
8 Bedroom

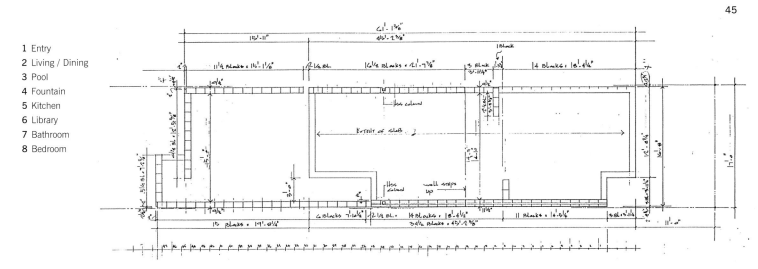

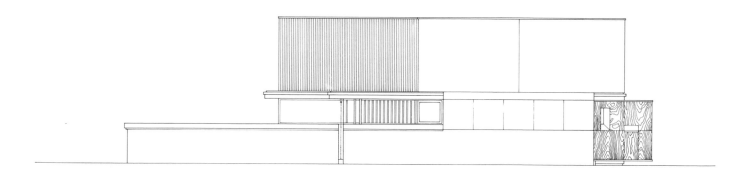

West Elevation

"The Laneway House construction drawings were hand drawn. It was a conventional contract with a general contractor and a site supervisor. The contractor built 80 percent of the house. To save money, we carried out the final 20 percent, where a high proportion of the total cost resides. We did most of the finishing work, including exterior siding, wood floors, interior painting and the skylight over the stair."

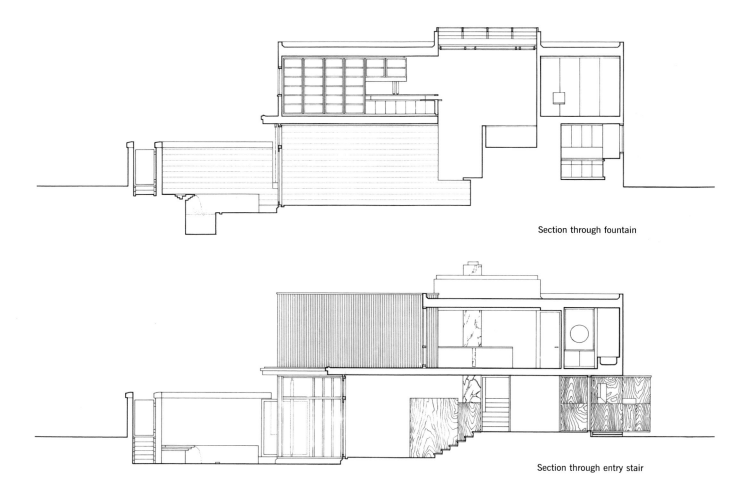

Section through fountain

Section through entry stair

48

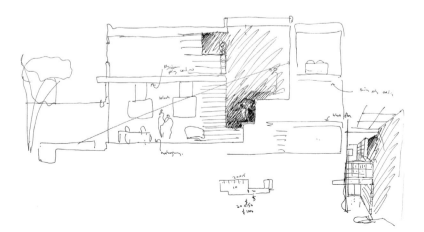

"The horizon line of the Laneway House is at the junction of the concrete block wall and the translucent clerestory. Moving from the entry, where this horizon line is just above eye level, we descend two feet to the main living and dining space. Through this change in section, the main space of the house is separated from the external world, yet connected directly to the courtyard garden."

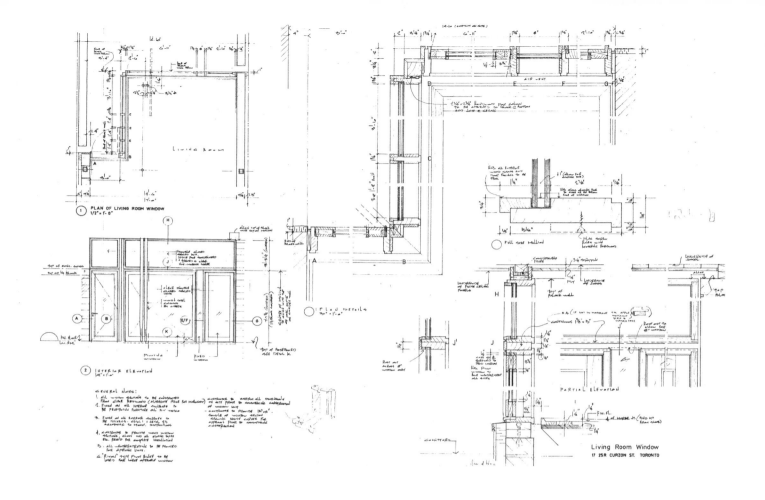

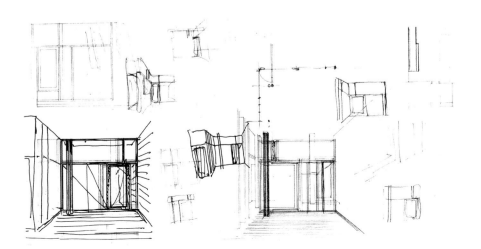

The window wall of the Laneway House integrates the living space and the courtyard garden in all seasons. When the 8 x 8 foot panel pivots open, the link is physical and seamless; when closed, the connection is visual. The window wall is folded in plan, pushing the living room out into the garden and, conversely, pulling the garden inside. Compositionally, two free-standing columns in the room echo the two similarly spaced mullions of the window, and etched glass windows form a continuous luminous band above.

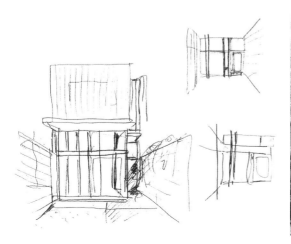

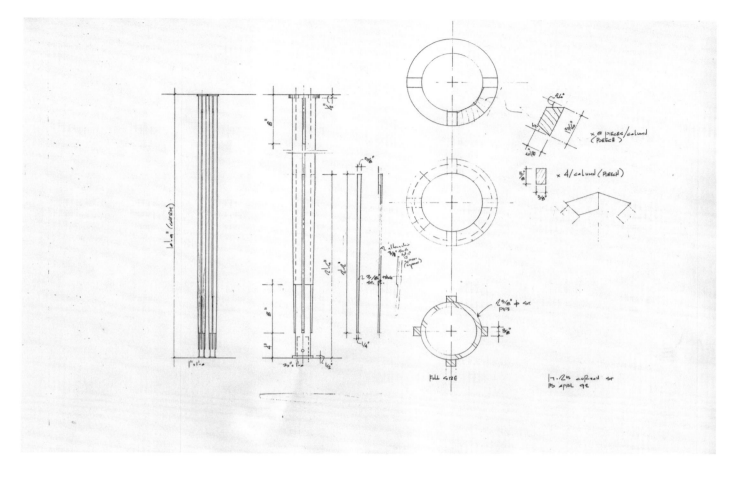

"The column is a significant architectural element in a number of our projects. The cluster of very slender columns of the Garden Pavilion was followed by the Laneway House, where the columns were inspired by the chromium clad columns of the Barcelona Pavilion and Tugendhat House by Ludwig Mies van der Rohe, and the clusters of wood columns in Alvar Aalto's Villa Mairea. Initially, the Laneway House columns were designed as steel pipes with welded steel blades and wood cladding. These evolved into a cruciform armature of standard steel angles and plates, with tapered mahogany cladding. The articulated column was further developed (left to right) in the Muskoka Boathouse, the house in Claremont, Corkin Gallery and the Integral House."

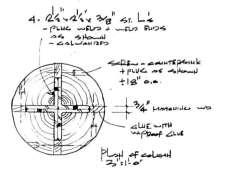

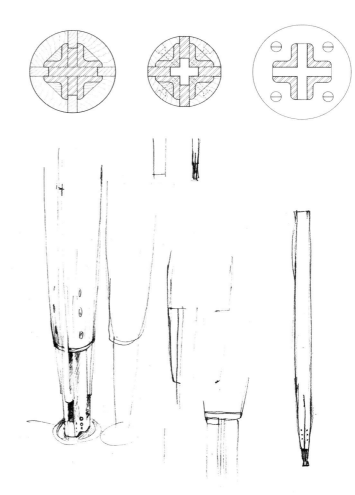

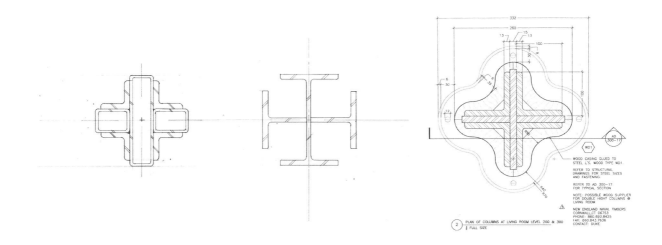

WOOD CASING GLUED TO
STEEL L'S. WOOD TYPE W01.

REFER TO STRUCTURAL
DRAWINGS FOR STEEL SIZES
AND FASTENING.

REFER TO AD 300-17
FOR TYPICAL SECTION

NOTE: POSSIBLE WOOD SUPPLIER
FOR DOUBLE HIGHT COLUMNS @
LIVING ROOM

NEW ENGLAND NAVAL TIMBERS
CORNWALL,CT 06753
PHONE: 860.893.8425
FAX: 860.843.7636
CONTACT: DUKE

2 PLAN OF COLUMNS AT LIVING ROOM LEVEL 200 & 300
½ FULL SIZE

"The handrails on the stair are recent additions, which we designed and installed in 2011. They are an expression of two types of detailing that we have developed for handrails.

The rail for the stair that goes down to the living room is a steel pipe rail with transitional steel rods. This language has developed through multiple projects: Corkin Gallery has steel pipe and transitional rods, all painted white. In the Weathering Steel House, we use Cor-Ten pipe, which we weathered ourselves by spraying it with water until it was a rich colour and then sealing it. The Cor-Ten pipe is combined with waxed steel rod and stainless steel mesh. This detail is elaborated in the Integral House, where pipe rails wrapped in leather are supported by cast bronze stanchions, and bronze framing holds a more complex stainless steel mesh."

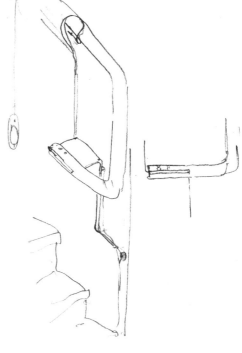

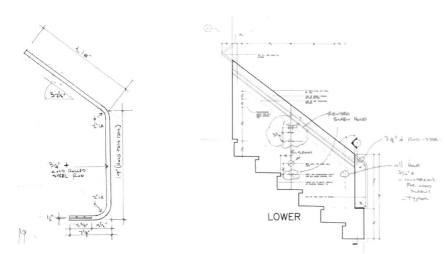

LOWER

"The stair to the upper floor explores a second type of handrail detailing that we developed more recently. It is a folded steel sheet that is partially embedded in the wall and plastered over, so that the handrail feels like an extension of the wall, which has been folded out. Our first use of this detail was for a dressing room and gallery in the Frum residence, which we designed in 2011. There the blued steel is waxed. In the Laneway House, the steel sheet is painted red."

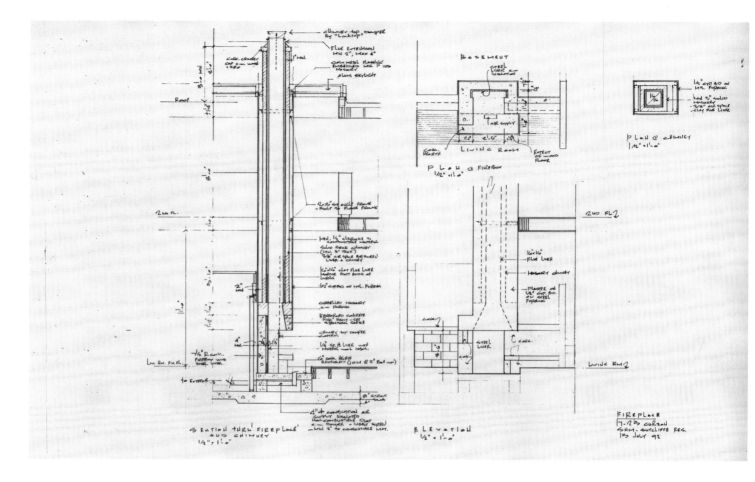

Fireplace technical drawings: *Section thru fireplace and chimney* (1/4" = 1'-0"), *Plan @ firebox* (1/2" = 1'-0"), *Plan @ chimney* (1/2" = 1'-0"), *Elevation* (1/2" = 1'-0"). Labeled "FIREPLACE — 17-123 CURZON — SHIM. SUTCLIFFE RES. — 15 JULY 92"

56

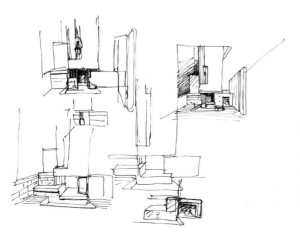

"Kurt Forster has suggested that the fireplace of the Laneway House is the first of a series of experiments in making miniature architecture. It is intentionally overscaled for such a small house. The site cast concrete hearth, like the exposed interior face of the concrete block walls, is grounded. In contrast, the chimney is a luminous floating volume at the center of the house. This light reflector is finished with creamy yellow polished plaster called Marmorino Veneziano. The workman, who had never done it before, was instructed by an Italian plasterer who lives in Toronto. He used a buffer normally used for waxing cars, and it worked very well. The steel grate was made by Joe and Mike Muma, the same fabricators who helped to build the roof of the Garden Pavilion. Following the Laneway House, the idea of the fireplace as miniature architecture was developed in the Weathering Steel House and the Integral House."

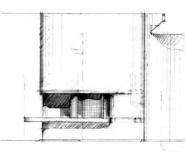

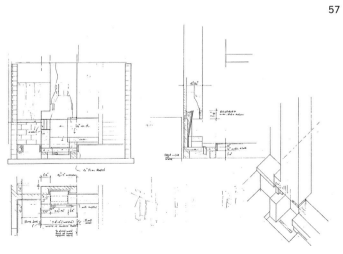

58

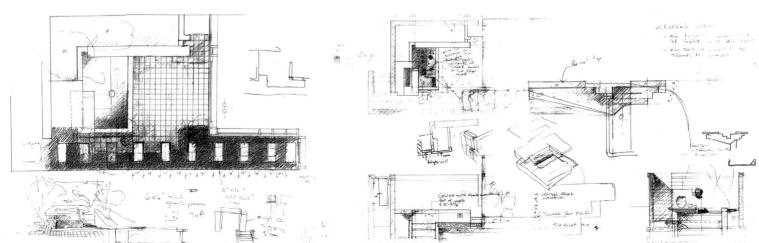

17-25 R. CURZON
25 SEPT 91

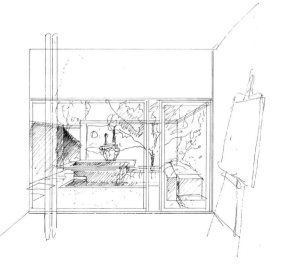

"The garden is a miniature cosmos, an idealized piece of nature in the city. It is enclosed by a concrete block wall, with an opening at the corner to reveal the world beyond. The garden is an experiment with water. As you walk down the laneway, you cannot see into the garden, but can hear the fountain. There are fish in the pool, and birds come all year round. The fountain runs throughout the year, and the movement of the water prevents it from freezing. Occasionally, if the weather is extremely cold — below -10 degrees Celsius — we use a small floating heater. At times during the winter, we look out through the glazed end of the house to see the water in the fountain and, at the same time, we can see the reflection of the fire in the glass."

Harrison Island Camp

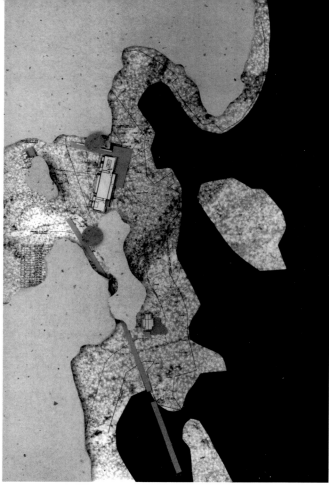

Georgian Bay, on the east side of Lake Huron, is nearly as large as the lake itself. Settled by Aboriginal peoples for thousands of years, it was revealed to Europeans by Samuel de Champlain in the early 1600s, who was followed by French missionaries. Today, Georgian Bay remains sparsely populated and relatively undeveloped. Harrison Island, one of the Thirty Thousand Islands on the east shore, is accessible in summer by boat from Bayfield Inlet on the mainland, and across the ice in winter.

65

The Canadian Shield covers half of the
landmass of Canada. This vast expanse
of lakes, swamps and Pre-Cambrian
igneous and metamorphic rock extends
from the Great Lakes to the Arctic Ocean
in the north. It is the ancient geological
core of North America that rose to
the surface and was exposed by the
retreat of the last glaciers. A thin layer
of topsoil, pierced by granite outcrops,
supports one of the largest tracts of
primeval forest in the world.

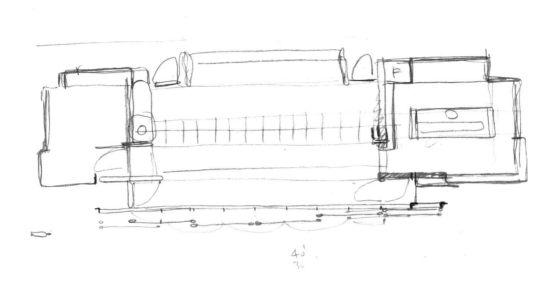

The plan organization of the Harrison Island Camp —
like the House on Henry's Meadow — is a bar flanked
by two thick zones on the long facades. The edge
zone on the landside houses a long built-in leather day
bed with a horizontal slot window above, while the
same zone on the waterside houses the entrance and
a long porch with sliding panels that enable it to be
both an interior and exterior space.

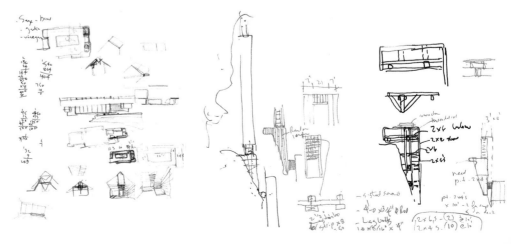

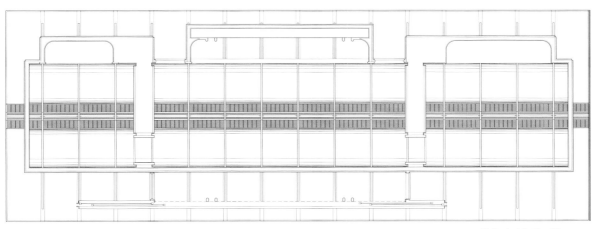

Reflected Ceiling Plan

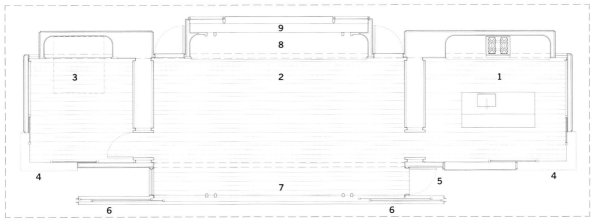

3

2

1

9

8

4

5

4

7

6

6

Floor Plan

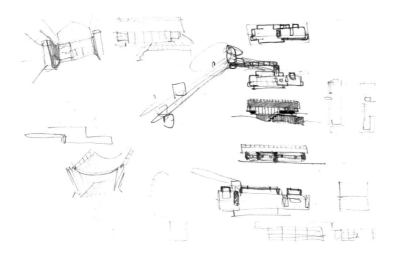

1 Kitchen
2 Living / Dining
3 Bedroom
4 Sliding corner windows,
   deep space and insect screens
5 Entry door
6 Translucent sliding panels
7 Rolling insect screens
8 Day bed
9 Bookshelves and window

0 1   5   10'

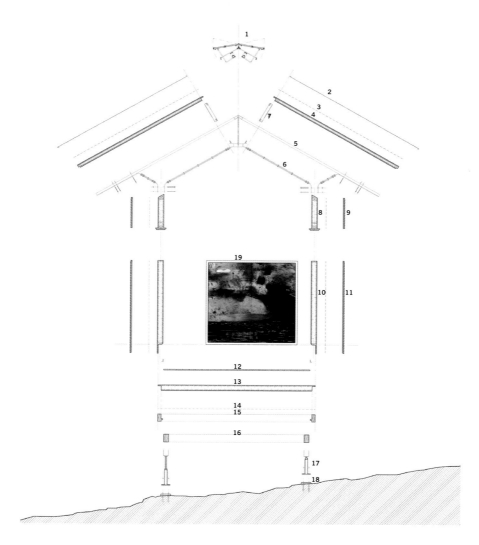

1. Operable greenhouse ridge skylight/vent with clear double skin acrylic panels
2. 16 gauge Cor-Ten steel roof screwed to 1 x 4 sleepers @ 16 inches O.C.
3. Roofing membrane
4. 2 ½ inch thick structural insulated panel (SIP) roof
   (½ inch plywood / 1 ½ inch rigid insulation / ½ inch plywood)
5. 2 x 3 inch hollow steel section rafters @ 48 inches O.C.
6. Steel frame 1 ¼ x 2 inch steel flat bar / ½ x 1 ½ inch steel flat bar /
   ¼ x 2 inch steel flat bar
7. Douglas Fir compression cord screen, 2 x 3 inch @ 8 inches O.C.
8. Continuous box beam supporting roof assembly (2 x 4 @ 16 inches O.C.,
   ¼ inch plywood / rigid insulation / ¼ inch plywood),
   ½ inch steel plate top and bottom
9. Wood cladding ¾ x 2 ¾ inch shiplap, stained black

10. 4 ½ inch thick structural insulated panel (SIP) wall
    (½ inch plywood / 3 ½ inch rigid insulation / ½ inch plywood)
    28 gauge galvanized metal
11. Wood cladding
12. Finished floor
13. 4 ½ inch thick structural insulated panels (SIP)
    (½ inch plywood / 3 ½ inch rigid insulation / ½ inch plywood)
14. 28 gauge galvanized metal finish glued to underside of ply
15. 2 x 8 joists @ 48 inches O.C.
16. Foundation beam 3 – 2 x 8
17. Adjustable steel jack posts bolted to rock
18. ½ inch diameter threaded rod anchors, epoxy into rock
19. Landscape painting: *Cloud Over Water,* Paterson Ewen, 1979

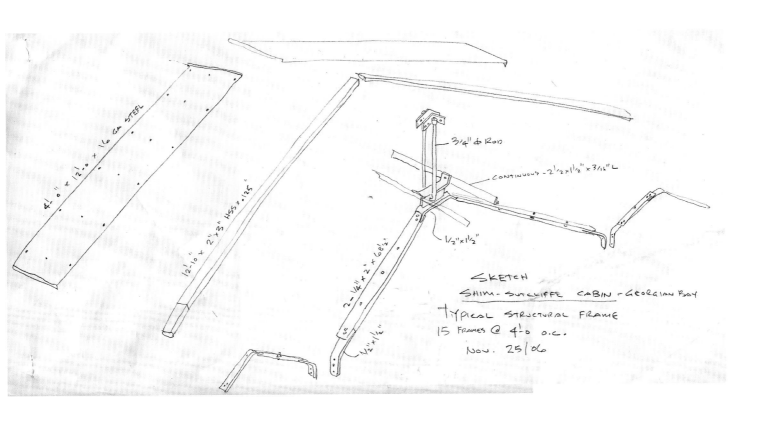

4'-0" x 12'-0" x 16 GA STEEL

12'-10" x 2"x3" HSS x .125"

3/4" Ø ROD

CONTINUOUS - 2½" x 1½" x 3/16" L

1/2" x 1½"

2 - ¼" x 2" x 26½"

½" x 1½"

SKETCH
SHIM - SUTCLIFFE CABIN - GEORGIAN BAY
TYPICAL STRUCTURAL FRAME
15 FRAMES @ 4'-0 O.C.
NOV. 25/06

"For the Harrison Island Camp, we worked with two principal fabricators — Tremonte Manufacturing for steel and Two Degrees North for joinery. Tremonte, a miscellaneous metals workshop, is headed by a former student of architecture at University of Toronto. Tremonte fabricated the weathering steel retaining wall for the Frum Memorial. The gate at the Frum Memorial was fabricated by Muma Manufacturing in St. Thomas, Ontario, a company that repairs farm equipment and welds gravel crushers. Muma fabricated the roof of the Garden Pavilion, and we returned to them for the memorial gate.

We subsequently worked with Tremonte Manufacturing on the Weathering Steel House and built a full size mock-up at their workshop. This enabled us to test the details — the thickness of the steel plate, the dimensions of the open joints, the design of the channel support system and, critically, the pattern of weathering and staining on the weathering steel cladding.

Our first project with Two Degrees North was for Jane Corkin, the client for the Corkin Gallery, who wanted a mirror for her home. The Eclipse Mirror that we designed was a small wood framed mirror with elements that folded out, like planets and moons. Two Degrees North subsequently did the interior joinery of the Weathering Steel House and several other commissions.

When we approached Tremonte and Two Degrees North to work with us on the Harrison Island Camp, we had shared knowledge and experience of collaboration on previous projects. Two Degrees North acted as general contractor, led by Jim Marshall. As with the Laneway House, we did most of the finishing ourselves."

"The images created by the Group of Seven represent a Canadian sensibility, which means that they contain in the choice of their subject, and in the means of expressing it, an essential reflection of who we are as individuals brought up in this particular part of the world.

….Thomson's great paintings *The West Wind* and *The Jack Pine* are the visual equivalent of a national anthem, for they have come to represent the spirit of the whole country…."

David P. Silcox, *The Group of Seven and Tom Thomson* (Toronto: Firefly Books Ltd) 2003, pp. 49–50.

Tom Thomson, Canadian (1877–1917)
The West Wind, winter 1916–1917
Oil on canvas. 47 1/2 x 54 5/16" (120.7 x 137.9 cm)
Art Gallery of Ontario, Gift of the Canadian Club of Toronto, 1926. 784

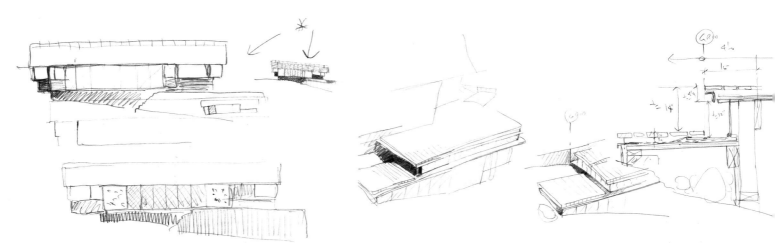

"From the floating boat dock of Harrison Island, we step onto granite rocks, which were exposed thousands of years ago by retreating glaciers, and then onto a long boardwalk that leads to the cabin. The boardwalk, which weaves between trees and is scribed carefully around the rocks, arrives in a clearing framed by the backs of two small buildings — the weathering steel cabin and the wood clad wash house. Both of these facades are closed, with only small openings overlooking the clearing. Continuing around the east end of the cabin, a view of the water opens up and the entrance to the cabin is revealed. Like the boardwalk, the cabin touches the ground in the most delicate way possible, with its elevated floor platform supported by scaffolding screw jacks that are anchored into the exposed bedrock of the Canadian Shield."

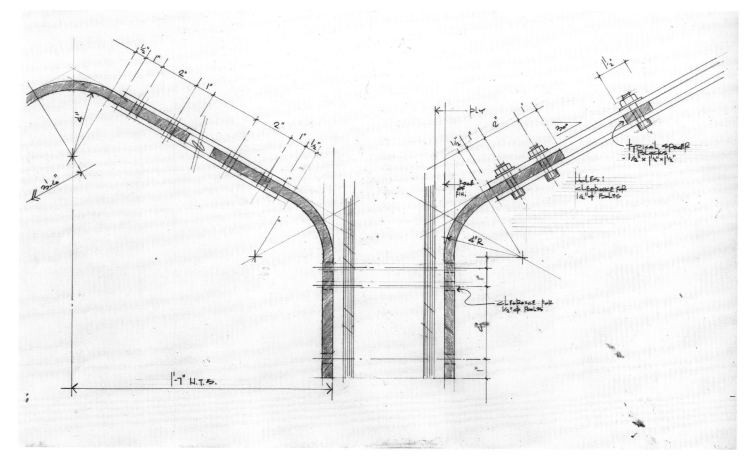

74

"In contrast with the custom designed structure of the Harrison Island Cabin, its skylight, a component developed for commercial glasshouses, is a standard off-the-shelf product. Our first use of this motorized industrial element was in the Moorelands Camp Dining Hall. It is operable, inexpensive and provides adjustable natural ventilation as well as ample daylight."

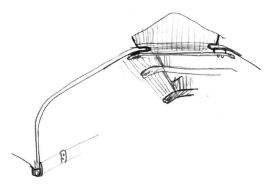

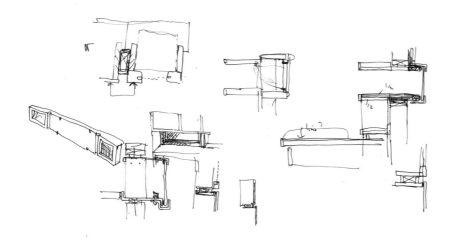

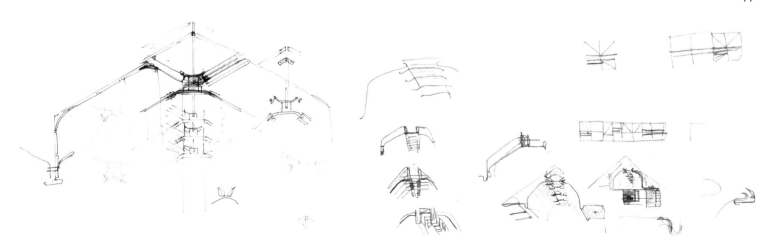

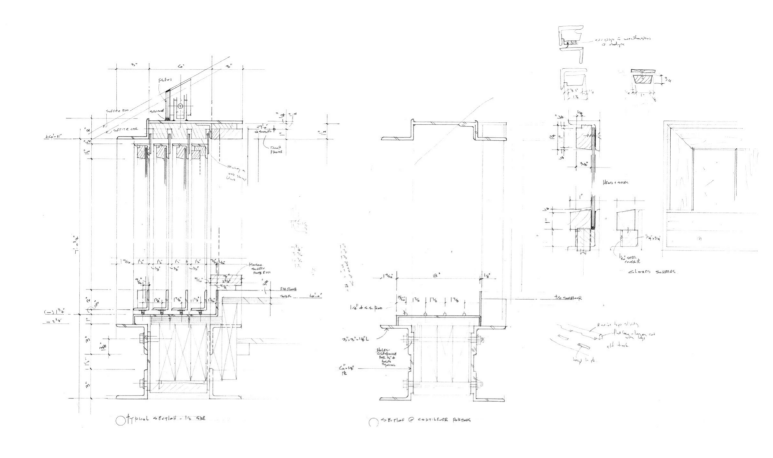

78

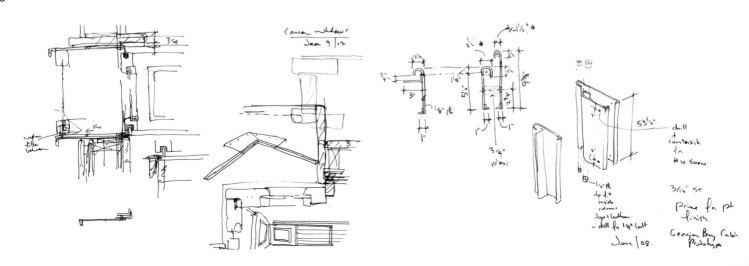

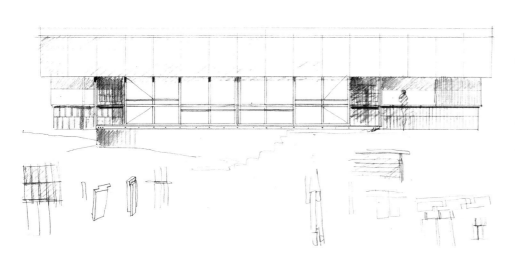

"In contrast with the north facing rear wall of the cabin, which is predominantly closed, the south façade has panoramic views looking out to Georgian Bay. Two layers of full height sliding panels — translucent fiberglass and insect screens — can be opened and closed to create a series of conditions that mediate between inside and outside, enabling us to both be exposed to and protected from nature."

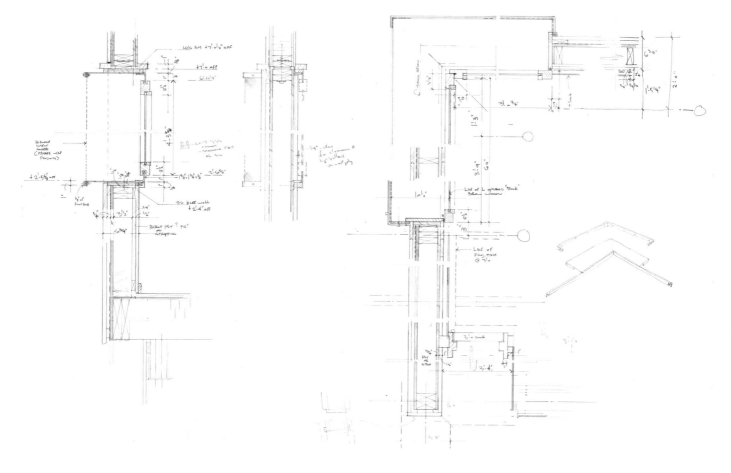

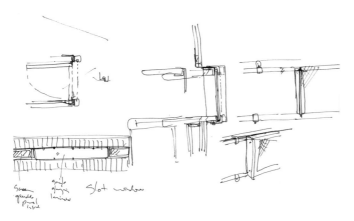

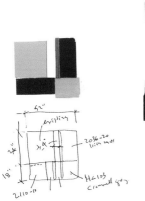

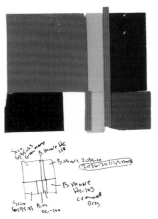

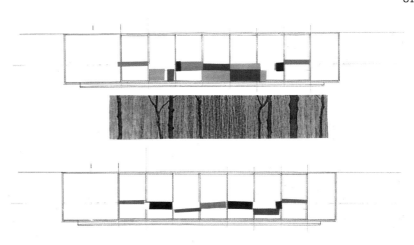

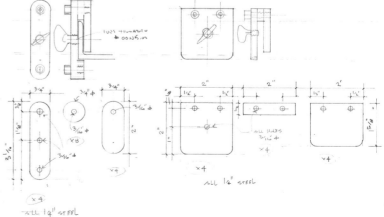

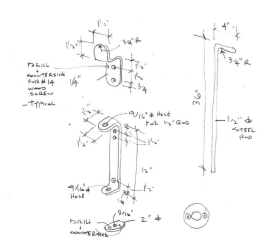

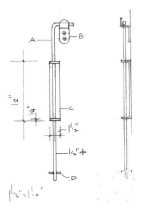

"For the ironmongery we have designed for a number of our projects, we have worked with many collaborators. Early in our practice, we met the artist Takashi Sakamoto. He is a master craftsman who is skilled in the use of steel, stainless steel, bronze and other metals. For the Muskoka Boathouse, we worked with him to develop prototypes for handles using folded plate and rods."

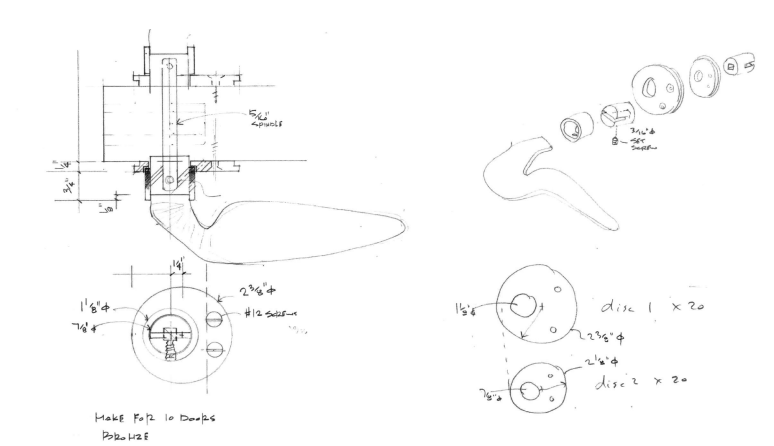

5/16"
SPINDLE

1/4"

3/4"

1/16"

1 4"

2 3/8" φ

#12 screws

1 1/8" φ

7/8"

MAKE FOR 10 DOORS
BRONZE

3/16" φ
SET
SCREW

1 1/8" φ

2 3/8" φ

disc 1 x 20

1 1/8" φ

7/8" φ

2 1/8" φ

disc 2 x 20

7/8" φ

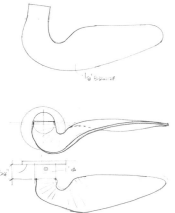

"By the time we designed the Integral House, we developed our own prototypes for door handles — initially in clay, then a series of 3-D printed versions. The final metal castings were made in the USA. At the same time that we were designing the Harrison Island Camp, we were working with MCM Toronto to fabricate metalwork for the Frum Collection of African Art at the Art Gallery of Ontario, where folded steel plate was heated in oil, then quenched to make it black. As a result, we worked with MCM to make door handles for the camp. For these, we also used steel plate, a material we had originally used with Sakamoto to make simple pulls for cupboard doors. Now, instead of folding, the plate was hammered into shape by a blacksmith. The surface consequently bears the marks of its making, giving the handles a rustic character."

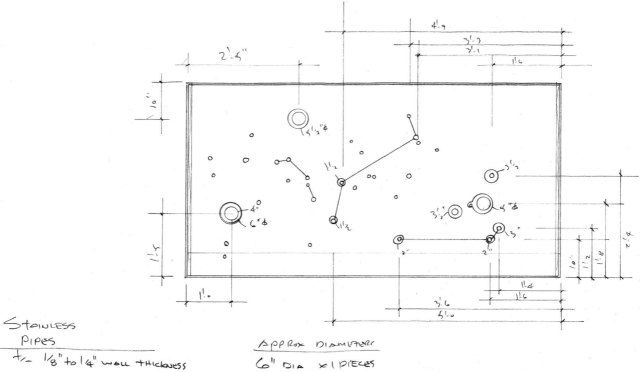

STAINLESS
PIPES
+/- 1/8" to 1/4" WALL THICKNESS
± 5" LONG
1 END FINISHED
to #4 FIN. LEVEL

APPROX DIAMETERS
6" DIA x 1 PIECES
5 1/2"   x 1
5"   x 1
4   x 1
3 1/2"   x 2
3"   x 1
2"   x 2
1 1/2"   x 2

"The "Night Sky" panel over the fireplace reflects an ongoing interest in understanding our place in nature. A collage of found objects — weathered plywood full of knots, nails and painted metal parts — transforms into a constellation, a representation of nature that is connected to this place. This panel is inspired by the collages of Joan Miro and the paintings of the late Paterson Ewen, a client and friend."

Joan Miro (1893–1983)
© Successió Miró / SODRAC (2014) © ARS, NY
Relief Construction, Montroig, August–November 1930
Oil on wood, nails, staples, and metal on wood panel.
35 7/8 x 27 5/8 x 6 3/8" (91.1 x 70.2 x 16.2 cm). Purchase.
Location: The Museum of Modern Art, New York, NY, USA

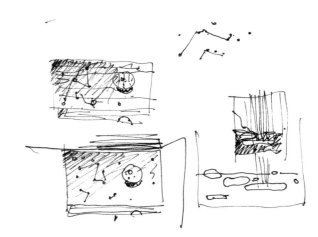

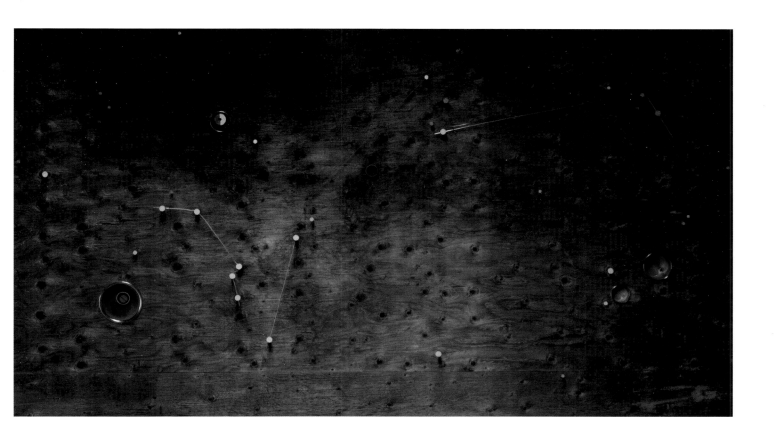

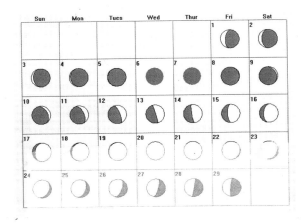

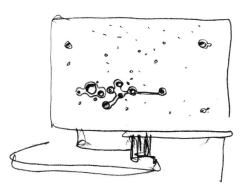

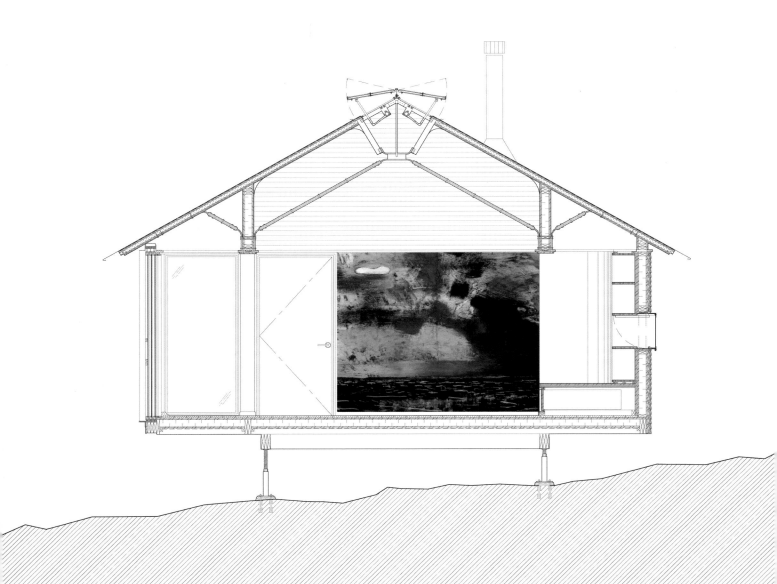

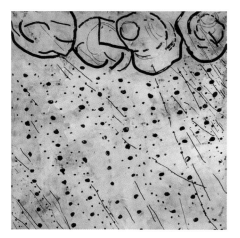

"Ewen makes his unorthodox "canvases" of huge sheets of plywood, which he scores and gouges with a router, adorns with pieces of metal and roughly paints. They have all the grandeur of elemental forces — the grooves transformed into impressionist crests of waves or windblown trails of sunlit clouds. It is as if Tom Thomson's *West Wind* was rerouted through the cosmic scale of Turner."

Philip Monk, "A '70s selection for export only." *Maclean's,*
29 September 1980, as cited in Matthew Teitelbaum (editor),
Paterson Ewen (Vancouver + Toronto: Douglas + McIntyre,
and Toronto: Art Gallery of Ontario) 1996, p. 143.

Paterson Ewen, Canadian (1925–2002)
Precipitation, 1973
Acrylic and metal on gouged plywood. 244.0 x 229.0 cm
Cloud Over Water, 1979 (opposite)
Acrylic and metal on gouged plywood. 224.0 x 335.0 cm
Collection: Art Gallery of Ontario

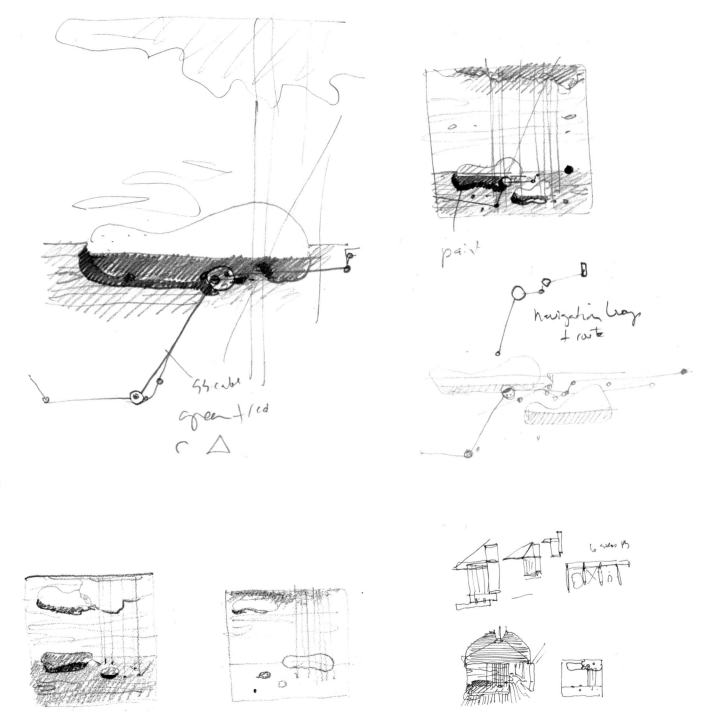

SS cube

green + red

c △

pair

Navigation loop
+ route

6 sides pg

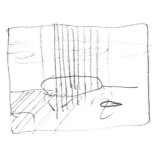

"At the east end of the living room is another collage of found objects called "Navigational Channels." Inspired by Japanese woodblock prints that depict rain so persuasively, this piece uses stainless steel wires that catch light from the skylight above to represent rain, together with weathering steel islands that float on a sea of weathered plywood."

Utagawa Hiroshige established landscape as a popular new genre of woodblock art in Japan. Hiroshige's prints were collected by European artists and influenced the work of the Impressionists. Frank Lloyd Wright organized a major exhibition of Hiroshige's work at the Art Institute of Chicago in 1906.

Utagawa Hiroshige (1797–1858)
Station 49, Spring Rain at Tsuchiyama.
The Fifty-Three Stations of the Tokaido, 1833–34
Public Domain. Photograph courtesy Shim-Sutcliffe Collection, 2013.

Reading the text and images of *The Passage of Time* I cannot help but be reminded constantly of Mies van der Rohe. The connection is not in the formal but in the process of design. Experimentation and the experimental are integral components of imaginatively committed design developed by architects who advance the field. Mies tested his experimental concepts through sketches that investigated all possible variations; the solutions chosen (usually not one but three) evolved through drawings and study models, and conclusions were further tested in full-scale mock-ups. And one experiment led to another. Similar studies of whole and part and detail may be seen in the work of the Scandinavian architects Sigurd Lewerentz and Alvar Aalto whom Shim and Sutcliffe value highly.

What is fascinating are the very different outcomes from similar design processes. The difference is in the approach and intention. Mies's approach is conceptual: he insisted on the generality of principles and the universality of architectural issues. Mies's basic statement about his work was "My idea, or better, 'direction,' in which I go is toward a clear structure and construction."[1] For Shim and Sutcliffe, the building is not unified by a single dominant architectural concept but lies, as it does in the work of Lewerentz and Aalto, in "a conglomeration of ideas, impressions and associations held together by a sensual atmosphere."[2] Issues that underlie and sustain the mediating aspects of design at the very centre of the concerns of Shim and Sutcliffe — purpose, function, and place that modulate the qualities of space and material — were subliminal for Mies.

Place is of consequence in the city house and the country house which are the subject of this book. Shim and Sutcliffe are concerned with intensifying land use in the city, incorporating "lush gardens" referring us to nature. In the northern wilderness they respond to strong natural forms. Other design concerns are abundant — the manipulation of light; combining architecture, landscape design and industrial design; experimentation with colour; and how a building meets the ground. Environmental stewardship is exquisitely present.

Postscript Phyllis Lambert

In sharp contrast, Mies was working on architecture as a language: "I think you have to have a grammar in order to have a language. You can use it for normal purposes and you speak in prose. And if you are good at that you speak a wonderful prose, and if you are really good you can be a poet."[3] Step by step Mies developed and refined the grammar from one project to another: at the Illinois Institute of Technology (IIT) Campus and in the language of the clear-span structure that he initiated at the Farnsworth House and expanded to the institutional scale at Crown Hall; in tall buildings, at 860-880 Lake Shore Drive, the steel skin with rolled steel mullions is virtually glued to the structure, then freed from the skeleton frame with the extruded bronze enclosure of the Seagram building. The concern is for structural clarity and refinement.

The reciprocities between projects that Shim and Sutcliffe consider to be fundamental to their work are sensual rather than structural. In discussing their very finely drawn Laneway House and the Harrison Island Camp in the context of the body of their work, they trace discovery of the play of light and the sense of movement occasioned by the thick wall from the Craven Road Studio, to the South Portland synagogue with its thick walls of light and shadow, from the Island Studio to the Integral House and further articulated in the institutional-scale Residence for the Sisters of Saint Joseph. They would certainly agree with Mies that "nature should also live its own life....We should attempt to bring nature, houses, and human beings together in a higher unity."[4] However, the idea of natural environment, which consciously permeates their work, is a sensibility of Canadians for whom raw nature is never far distant. The presence of ravines in Toronto and the wilderness of Georgian Bay impresses the way Shim and Sutcliffe site buildings, and when necessary they create a landscape.

One could continue thinking of the universal versus specificity, the abstract versus figuration, the comparison of object and process, the transcendent sense of architecture, attention to detail and all elements of design, materiality, off-the-shelf structural steel versus break formed plates and rods, and so on. Thinking of Mies sharpens sensibilities to the work of Shim and Sutcliffe.

1. Mies van der Rohe to Cameron Alread, Edow Davidson, Edgar Marshall, and Louis Thomas, May 11, 1960, Ludwig Mies van der Rohe Papers, container 54, Manuscript Division, Library of Congress.
2. Thomas W. Ryan, "Horizontal Light: Lewerentz, Aalto and the Nordic Landscape," accessed April 23, 2014. http://archleague.org/2013/03/horizontal-light-lewerentz-aalto-and-the-nordic-landscape-by-thomas-ryan/
3. Mies van der Rohe, transcript of interview with John Peter, 1955, 4. Interviews with Ludwig Mies van der Rohe, Mies Papers, container 62, Manuscript Division, Library of Congress.
4. Mies van der Rohe quoted in Fritz Neumeyer, *The Artless Word: Mies van der Rohe and the Building Art,* trans. Mark Jarzombek (Cambridge: The MIT Press), 1991, p. 339.

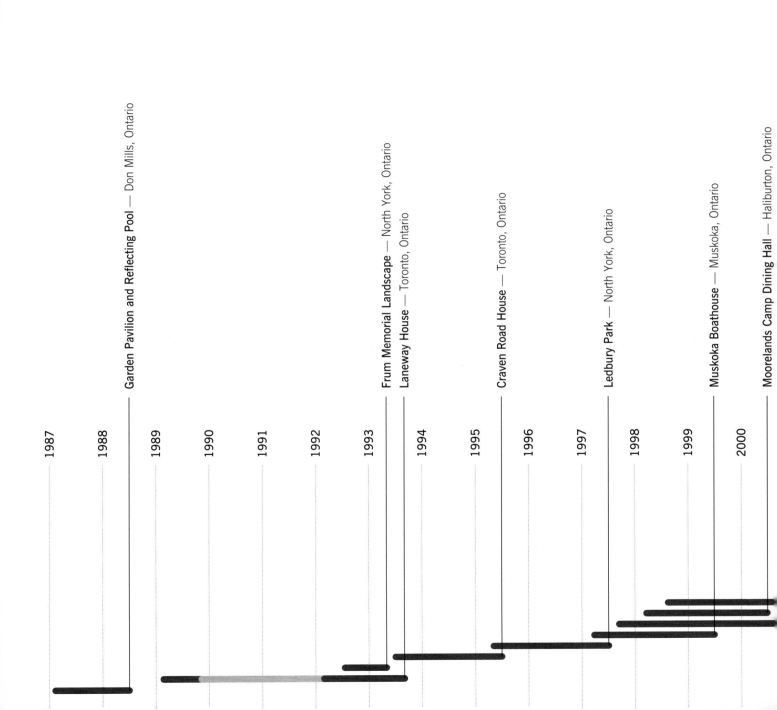

Garden Pavilion and Reflecting Pool — Don Mills, Ontario

Frum Memorial Landscape — North York, Ontario

Laneway House — Toronto, Ontario

Craven Road House — Toronto, Ontario

Ledbury Park — North York, Ontario

Muskoka Boathouse — Muskoka, Ontario

Moorelands Camp Dining Hall — Haliburton, Ontario

1987

1988

1989

1990

1991

1992

1993

1994

1995

1996

1997

1998

1999

2000

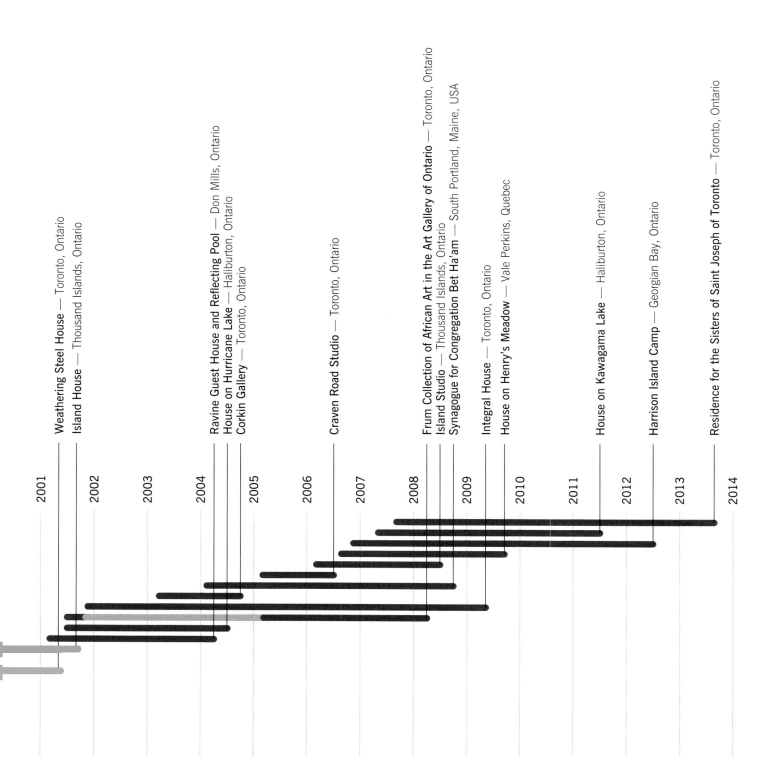

Weathering Steel House — Toronto, Ontario
Island House — Thousand Islands, Ontario

Ravine Guest House and Reflecting Pool — Don Mills, Ontario
House on Hurricane Lake — Haliburton, Ontario
Corkin Gallery — Toronto, Ontario

Craven Road Studio — Toronto, Ontario

Frum Collection of African Art in the Art Gallery of Ontario — Toronto, Ontario
Island Studio — Thousand Islands, Ontario
Synagogue for Congregation Bet Ha'am — South Portland, Maine, USA

Integral House — Toronto, Ontario
House on Henry's Meadow — Vale Perkins, Quebec

House on Kawagama Lake — Haliburton, Ontario

Harrison Island Camp — Georgian Bay, Ontario

Residence for the Sisters of Saint Joseph of Toronto — Toronto, Ontario

2001
2002
2003
2004
2005
2006
2007
2008
2009
2010
2011
2012
2013
2014

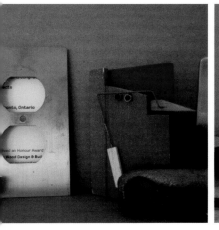  

Brigitte Shim was born in Kingston, Jamaica in 1958. Educated at the University of Waterloo, she received degrees in Environmental Studies and Architecture. She worked in Vancouver with Arthur Erickson and Associates and in Toronto with Baird/Sampson Architects. She is an Associate Professor at the John H. Daniels Faculty of Architecture, Landscape and Design at the University of Toronto where she has been teaching since 1988. She has held a number of Distinguished Visiting Professorships at Yale University and has been a Distinguished Visiting Critic at the University at Buffalo, and a Visiting Professor at Harvard's Graduate School of Design and the Ecole Polytechnique Federale de Lausanne. In 2007, she was a member of the Aga Khan Architecture Award master jury.

Howard Sutcliffe was born in Yorkshire, England in 1958. A graduate of the University of Waterloo, he holds degrees in Environmental Studies and Architecture. Prior to opening the Shim·Sutcliffe studio in 1994, he worked with Paul Merrick in Vancouver and Ronald Thom and Barton Myers Associates in Toronto. Subsequently, he worked for Kuwabara Payne McKenna Blumberg Architects, where he played a key role on award winning competition schemes including the Kitchener City Hall. He was the first recipient of the Ronald J. Thom Award for Early Design Achievement from Canada Council for the Arts.

The work of Shim·Sutcliffe has been published internationally and has received numerous awards, including thirteen Governor General's Medals and Awards for Architecture from the Royal Architectural Institute of Canada and a National Honor Award from the American Institute of Architects. Brigitte Shim and Howard Sutcliffe are Fellows of the Royal Architectural Institute of Canada, Honorary International Fellows of the American Institute of Architects and elected members of the Royal Canadian Academy. In 2013, they were awarded the Queen Elizabeth II Diamond Jubilee Medal and the Order of Canada.

Shim·Sutcliffe

Essy Baniassad, Dalhousie Professor Emeritus, founded Tuns Press in 1990 when he was Dean of the Faculty of Architecture at the Technical University of Nova Scotia. His research and teaching include architectural and urban design, theory and criticism and architectural education.

Brian Carter worked with Arup and was Chair of Architecture at the University of Michigan and Dean of the School of Architecture & Planning at the University at Buffalo, The State University of New York, where he is currently Professor of Architecture. Author of several books, he has curated exhibitions on Eero Saarinen, Albert Kahn and Peter Rice.

Phyllis Lambert — RAIC Gold Medalist, architect, author, lecturer, scholar, curator, citizen activist and critic of architecture and urbanism — is Founding Director Emeritus of the Canadian Centre for Architecture (CCA) in Montreal. Lambert is recognized internationally for her contribution in advancing contemporary architecture and her concern for the social issues of architecture and the role of architecture in the public realm.

Annette W. LeCuyer trained at the Architectural Association and worked in London prior to joining the faculty at the University of Michigan. A Professor of Architecture at the University at Buffalo, The State University of New York, she is a contributor to architectural journals and author of books on technology and design.

Christian Unverzagt co-founded M1/DTW, a Detroit based design studio engaged in the material production of objects, artifacts, identities and spaces, in 2000. He is an Assistant Professor of Practice in Architecture at the University of Michigan Taubman College.

102 **Contributors**

This publication in the *Documents in Canadian Architecture* series is the result of the commitment and collaboration of many people. It is a reflection of the extraordinary energy and inspiration of Brigitte Shim and Howard Sutcliffe and the sustained development of their practice. Thanks are due to all of the people who have worked and those currently working in the office. During the preparation of this book, Ryan Beecroft, Roxane Bejjany and Andrew Hart have provided valuable assistance.

Essy Baniassad, who initiated the publications at Tuns Press, continues to enthusiastically help build this series of books on new architecture in Canada. Christine Macy, Dean of the School of Architecture and Planning at Dalhousie University, has provided support and prompted the recent transformation of Tuns Press through the creation of the Dalhousie Architectural Press. Professor Diogo Burnay, Director of Architecture, has consistently supported the publications. The assistance of staff in the School of Architecture & Planning, in particular Martha Barnstead and Don Westin, has been vital.

The Canadian Centre for Architecture has facilitated access to archival material. The support of Phyllis Lambert has been invaluable. Mary Hanford generously provided access to the work of Paterson Ewen, and David P. Silcox gave valuable guidance on the Group of Seven. The Museum of Modern Art in New York, in particular the assistance of Diana Pulling in liaising with the Miro Foundation, is much appreciated. We are grateful for the cooperation of the photographers who have recorded the work of Shim·Sutcliffe.

Annette W. LeCuyer and Brian Carter acknowledge the support of the Dean and Chair of Architecture at the School of Architecture & Planning at the University at Buffalo, The State University of New York. Special thanks are due to Christian Unverzagt and others at M1/DTW — Kristen Dean, Michael Sklenka and Eva Zielinski — for their assistance.

Acknowledgements & Credits

DRAWINGS:
Printed from drawings from *Site Unseen* (Toronto: University of Toronto Faculty of Architecture, Landscape and Design) 2004: 42.
Kyle Baptista/Toronto Park People: 10.
Printed from a photomechanical transfer; original drawings or works in the collection of the Centre Canadien d'Architecture / Canadian Centre for Architecture, Montreal: 43 lower, 44, 48 lower, 48 upper, 49, 50, 51, 52, 52, 53 upper, 56, 56 lower right, 57, 58, 59. © Shim-Sutcliffe Architects.

All other drawings and photographs courtesy Shim-Sutcliffe Architects.

PHOTOGRAPHS:
Michael Awad: 31.
Courtesy B+H Architects: 11.
Edward Burtynsky: 54 lower right.
James Dow: 12 right, 13, 14, 17 right, 18 right, 19, 20, 23, 27, 28, 29 right, 34, 38 left, 38 center, 47 upper, 51 upper, 54 upper left, 57, 73 upper right, 74, 81 upper right, 82, 83.
Steven Evans: 12 left, 43 upper, 51 lower.
Courtesy M. Gerhardt Real Estate Limited: 64.
Bob Gundu: 21, 26.
Courtesy Mary Hanford: 68, 90, 91 lower.
Eirik Johnson: 37.
Raimund Koch: 15.

Steve Moretti: 33.
Digital Image © The Museum of Modern Art/Licensed by SCALA / Art Resource, NY: 88.
Finn O'Hara: 29 left.
OMNR, Ontario Centre of Remote Sensing: 24.
© Queen's Printer for Ontario, 1984.
Positive and Imaging Photography: 22.
Simon Sutcliffe: 62, 76 upper, 79, 89, 91, 93, 94.
Christian Unverzagt: 100, 101.

All reasonable efforts have been made to identify owners of copyrights. Any errors or omissions will be corrected in future editions.